ZERO PREP FOR BEGINNERS

Ready-to-Go Activities for the Language Classroom

by
Laurel Pollard
Natalie Hess
Jan Herron

Credits

Acquisitions Editor: **Aarón Berman**
Production Editor: **Jamie A. Cross**
Interior Design: **Martie Sautter**
Cover Art: **Bruce Marion Illustration and Design**
Interior Art: **Kathleen Peterson**

Alta Book Center Publishers—San Franscisco
14 Adrian Court
Burlingame, California 94010 USA
Phone: 800 ALTA/ESL • 650.692.1285 (Int'l)
Fax: 800 ALTA/FAX • 650.692.4654 (Int'l)
Email: info@altaesl.com
Website: www.altaesl.com

Printed in the United States of America
ISBN 1-882483-82-0

DEDICATIONS

Laurel dedicates this book
To Geneva and Adam, who point the way.
To Dan, who shows me that the kayak *wants* to move forward—all you have to do is stroke the water.
To Jackie, my second self.

Natalie dedicates this book
To my girlfriends Juel and Carrie, who first heard me stumble in English—and survived.

Jan dedicates this book
To Suzannah, who thinks it's neat that her mom wrote a book.

ACKNOWLEDGMENTS

To everyone who mentored us, roped us in, egged us on, and told us we could do it.
To teachers of beginning language learners, who need stuff that works.

CONTENTS

INTRODUCTION 1

INTRODUCTION 2

INTRODUCTION 3

CHAPTER ONE: LISTENING

YOU'LL FIND MORE GOOD LISTENING ACTIVITIES IN THESE OTHER CHAPTERS:

CHAPTER TWO: SPEAKING

YOU'LL FIND MORE GOOD SPEAKING ACTIVITIES IN THESE OTHER CHAPTERS:

CHAPTER THREE: READING

YOU'LL FIND MORE GOOD READING ACTIVITIES IN THESE OTHER CHAPTERS:

CHAPTER FOUR: WRITING

YOU'LL FIND MORE GOOD WRITING ACTIVITIES IN THESE OTHER CHAPTERS:

CHAPTER FIVE: VOCABULARY

YOU'LL FIND MORE GOOD VOCABULARY ACTIVITIES IN THESE OTHER CHAPTERS:

CHAPTER SIX: STRUCTURE

YOU'LL FIND MORE GOOD GRAMMAR ACTIVITIES IN THESE OTHER CHAPTERS:

GENERAL INDEX OF ACTIVITIES

ALPHABETICAL INDEX OF ACTIVITIES

INTRODUCTION 1: THIS BOOK

(for people who have no time to read introductions to new books)

What if you took the time to mentally review every activity for beginning students that you had ever used or heard of, choosing only the activities that are the very best ones for language learning? What if you then selected from that collection only those activities that take <u>no</u> <u>time</u> for the teacher to prepare?

> We did that.
>
> Here it is.
>
> Enjoy!

INTRODUCTION 2: WHY A BOOK FOR BEGINNING STUDENTS?

The Original *Zero Prep*

Does this idea sound familiar? You may have seen our other book, the original *Zero Prep: Ready-to-Go Activities for the Language Classroom*. In the three years since it was published, many teachers have requested a similar book geared to the needs of beginning language students. This is it!

What's Different About Beginners?

We love working with beginners! They are often full of excitement because every week, they can do things in their new language that they couldn't do a week earlier.

We know this excitement may not be there at first for all students. Perhaps you're teaching a required foreign language class, and the students aren't especially eager to be there.

Whether your students are eager from the start—or reluctant at first—you want to offer them wonderful lessons without exhausting yourself.

Zero Prep for Beginners can make all the difference! It will help you spend less time on chores and give you more time for creativity, planning, and vision. We have included classic activities as well as innovative activities, all proven in years of classroom use to capture students' attention, increase motivation, and maximize learning.

Beginning students offer particular challenges to teachers:

- Beginners cannot yet create new language, but they can recreate and reformulate language that they encounter. In other words, they need plenty of input. The activities in *Zero Prep for Beginners* give you many ways to provide language input, including routines for using readings, dictations, pictures, actions, and songs to convey meaning.

- Because everything in the new language is a mystery at first, many beginners worry too much about making mistakes. They need to know that this classroom is safe. It helps if they know that their teacher and classmates know them and like them. This is why *Zero Prep for Beginners* includes activities that help students get to know one another. (See the list of "class cohesion" activities in the General Index.)

- Beginners find comfort in repetition. When so much is unknown, it helps to have familiar classroom routines, activities they know how to do because they have done them before. (More on this crucial idea of "routines" later.)

- It is particularly important for beginning students to understand that everyone will be making mistakes (*cheerfully* making mistakes!) and learning together in the process. When interest in an activity is high and the challenge level is just right, students are amazed at how much language they can produce! This is why *Zero Prep for Beginners* includes many activities that activate students. (See "Concentric Circle Talk," Chapter 2, page 32.)

- A student who is continually corrected by the teacher may become discouraged, yet students do need to know what is correct and what is not in their new language. *Zero Prep for Beginners* includes carefully controlled activities that lead students to correct uses of the language.

- When students do make mistakes—especially beginning students—it is tempting to jump in and help. But we must be sure not to do too much for them. We can give them good "shoes," but they must do the walking themselves. When our students discover and correct their own errors, they gain more confidence and pride. With well-designed activities, even beginners can do this! The peer-checking and self-checking activities in *Zero Prep for Beginners* develop students' own correctness "monitors," helping them to find their own errors and take charge of their own learning. (See "Revision: I Can Do It Myself!" Chapter 4, page 60, and "I Challenge!" Chapter 1, page 17)

- Carefully structured activities for group work help beginning students accomplish more than they could do alone. Group activities also promote the atmosphere of cooperation and community that we strive for in language classrooms. However, there comes a time when the individual must move away from the group and produce his/her own work, experiencing that "I can do it myself!" thrill of accomplishment. The activities in this book will help you to facilitate both group and individual work.

Stress and the Teacher

Language teaching is stressful work. We are constantly in front of people, yet, as we close the classroom door, we often feel very alone. We work in rooms next to colleagues, but we seldom work closely together on the problems we face. People often compare our work to that of actors, but we not only have to perform, we also have to write the script, set the stage, direct both the performers and the audience, write the reviews (as we think about the lesson once it's over) and critique the actors and the audience.

We wear many hats. Sometimes we feel like psychologists, sometimes like social workers. Sometimes we are like parents or older brothers and sisters. Sometimes (although most of us don't really like it) we have to behave like police officers.

Our students frequently tell us what to do ("Correct all my mistakes, please!"), and then they are profoundly unhappy if we actually do it. Students, administrators, and parents often have unrealistic goals ("I want to get rid of my foreign accent."), and they may blame us for not reaching the unreachable.

Our classes are invariably heterogeneous and multilevel. No matter how much we accomplish, there is always much more to be done.

How can we handle all this? Read on!

Planning vs. Preparation

We make a distinction between *planning* and *preparation*. *Planning* is always necessary. It's the long-range thinking we must do about what our students need and how we can help them achieve their goals.

Preparation is what a teacher needs to do to get a particular lesson ready for class—the daily grind of little chores, of handouts and quizzes and paper grading and inventing activities . . .

We know from our own experience as classroom teachers the exhaustion that comes from spending too many hours in lesson preparation.

This is especially true for beginning-level teachers. We have taught at all levels, and we find that we do more preparation for a beginning class. Beginners need more input, more frequent changes of activity, and more carefully planned recycling than more advanced students do. They are also less able to work independently.

Using this book will help you spend less time on the "chores" of preparation and give you more time for creativity, planning, and vision.

Routines

A unique feature of the *Zero Prep* books is our emphasis on classroom routines. A "routine," as we use the word, is an activity so effective, so flexible, that we find ourselves using it again and again, varying the content and level but keeping the basic structure of the activity intact.

We think of a routine as a cooking pot. You can use a pot for the preparation of all kinds of wonderful dishes, but you do need the pot, and the pot always remains the same.

Students, especially beginners, love routines because they feel they are on familiar ground: "I know how to do this!" Relieved of the need to figure out what they're supposed to do, they can plunge right in, giving all their attention to using their new language to do the job at hand.

And routines don't become boring because they are easy to vary in content, in level, and in the details of how we structure the activity. An old routine filled with new content offers both the kind of challenge and the kind of confidence beginning students need to move from the well-known to the unknown.

Most of the activities in this book are routines. Using them has simplified our work enormously, made us more confident as teachers, and made our classes more student-centered. We hope that you will use these routines frequently to meet the needs of your beginning students.

Easy to Use

A book designed to save you time needs to be easy to use. Like us, you probably have resource books sitting unused on your shelves because you can't find the activities you need quickly enough. Following are the features that will make *Zero Prep for Beginners* your quick and easy source for ideas.

The Chapters

There are times when you know you want to emphasize a particular skill, so the table of contents groups activities as *Listening*, *Speaking*, *Reading*, *Writing*, *Vocabulary*, and *Structure*. However, many activities are multi-skill. "Dictacomp," for example, combines dictation and composition; will you find it in *Listening* or in *Writing*?

Here's our solution: we decided on each activity's primary aim and put it in that chapter.

For example, in the table of contents, "Listening Dictacomp" is in Chapter 4, *Writing*. Since it's also an excellent listening activity, you will find it listed again in the bottom half of Chapter 1, *Listening*, after this sentence:

"You'll find more good listening activities in these other chapters."

4.1 Listening Dictacomp 48

No matter what skill you're aiming for, the table of contents makes it easy for you to find all the activities you need.

The Indexes

There are times when you need an activity that accomplishes a certain function or uses a particular resource. The "General Index" guides you to activities for these purposes (see page 129).

What if you know the name of an activity, "Gossip," for example, but have forgotten which chapter it's in? Turn to the "Alphabetical Index," and you'll find it in a moment (see page 147).

The Linkage Symbol

There are certain activities that you may want to do in sequence during a lesson. (For example, it works well to do "Listening Dictacomp" after "Reporter/Writer.") Where we have noticed such natural pairings, we've put this symbol by them so they're easy to spot.

The Teacher's Tool Kit

Most of the activities in this book need no special materials, but beginners do need more visual input than other students.

Your most important resource will be a picture file. You will want pictures in category sets (for example: foods, articles of clothing, other sets of vocabulary you want to teach). Keep on hand magazines and catalogs with pictures in them for students to cut out. Make sure you have a variety of pictures; have some pictures with many objects in them, and have other pictures that are large enough for the whole class to see.

Several activities will call for these supplies:

> crayons or colored markers
>
> a small bag for collecting slips of paper
>
> tape
>
> glue
>
> scissors
>
> a soft ball (easy to throw and catch)

The following supplies are called for by only one activity in the book:

> peanut butter, bread, a knife (another food may be substituted)
>
> folders with two pockets
>
> token prizes (small stones or candies)
>
> money (coins and bills)
>
> a scarf or piece of cloth to cover a student's eyes
>
> a bag full of school supplies (for example: stapler, pen, pencil, envelope, ruler, eraser, tape, paper clips, glue, push pins, computer disks)

As often as possible, add interest to a lesson by bringing in real objects, such as toy animals (plastic or stuffed fabric), plastic food, articles of clothing, or other examples of words you are teaching.

Note for Teachers of Languages Other Than English

The activities in this book are suitable for teaching any language. For the sake of convenience, and to make the book accessible to as many teachers as possible, the examples are in English.

INTRODUCTION 3: WHO WE ARE AND WHY WE WROTE THIS BOOK

We wrote this book to help ourselves and our colleagues become better teachers. We are sure that you share the love of our work, but that you, like many other language teaching professionals, would like the job to be more enjoyable and less stressful.

Laurel's Story: Back from the Brink of Burnout

Laurel's experience with beginners reflects why we lose too many good teachers to burnout. Here is her story:

I started teaching beginners right out of graduate school. I loved it! At last I had my own class of eager learners. I used a modified audio-visual approach with filmstrips and dialogues, preparing every lesson carefully and staying up late each night to revise the plans for the next day. The students made remarkable progress—and I progressed rapidly toward burnout, feeling more exhausted as time went on. In my third year of teaching, I was assigned to a more advanced level. Sorry as I was to leave my beginners, I realized that I couldn't have kept that up for much longer.

When I returned to teaching beginners years later, it was a different story. I had learned that well-designed zero-prep routines allow even beginners to take a more active hand in their own learning, giving the teacher time to think and to breathe. I began inventing and collecting activities like "Revision: I Can Do It Myself!" Chapter 4, page 60, that have saved many teachers the frustration of continually correcting the same errors by empowering students to "make new errors, not old ones!"

Natalie's Story: The Students Who "Couldn't" Learn

Natalie had taught advanced students for many years when she was suddenly faced with a class of frustrated beginners. These were teenagers who had tried to learn the target language (English, in this case) many times and failed. Here is her story:

I instantly felt their frustration and anger. At first I had no idea what to do with these students. Then I solved their initial discomfort by talking to them in their native language, telling them that they actually already knew many words in English. They rather doubted me until I offered them examples like "television" and "telephone." Suddenly the students came alive. In groups, on very large pieces of paper, they wrote down all the words that they already knew in English. Among the words on their soon-very-full papers were words like *McDonald's, hamburger, hot dog, salad, autobus, automobile, doctor, ambulance, Coca Cola, Kleenex, bubble gum, film, nylon, grill, chicken, beauty queen, breaks, ski, pool,* and *ice cream*. Once they had posted the word-papers around the room and had a chance to explain the words to their classmates, English didn't seem like such a forbidden territory, and the class could move on to things like self introductions and greetings. This activity became one of my *Zero Prep* routines. (It is called "All the Words We Know," Chapter 5, page 68.)

A positive atmosphere and a feeling of trust and "can-do" are elements of great importance in all language classes, but especially so in classes of beginners. This activity activated the students, used their prior knowledge, helped them to move on to other language skills, helped them to create a sense of community, and, best of all, took no preparation whatsoever.

Jan's Story: Bridging the Great Divide

Jan had plenty of experience teaching beginners. Then her school accepted students from a very different educational background. Suddenly her class was much more "multilevel" than it had ever been before! Here's Jan's story:

My first class as an ESL teacher was a group of beginning learners. Being new at the job, I was naïve enough not to realize that I was probably given that class because nobody else wanted to teach beginners. One of my colleagues once told me, "I like students who can understand my jokes." Another said, "I like to be able to say something once and be understood." These things just cannot be done in a class of beginners.

Well, I was new and excited, and I desperately wanted to be a good teacher, so I read everything I could lay my hands on, and I learned as much as I could as fast as I could. And then the miracle happened—the confusion I had seen on the faces of my students was being replaced with understanding. Just as I was realizing, "Yes, I can do this!" My students were finding that, "Yes, we can use this new language."

Years passed. I was now an experienced teacher with an extensive repertoire of activities and classroom strategies, when suddenly things changed. My school accepted a large group of older, non-English-speaking, working-class people who had lost their jobs and needed to improve their English for job training. They had had limited access to formal education, some having gone no farther than the third grade. How was I to teach them in the same class with my university-bound international students?

I had to look at every activity with a new eye. What could I use? What would I need to do before it? How could I split it into beginning and very easy beginning? How much would I have to recycle? How could students do an activity together, each at their own level? The new students were very uncomfortable, even afraid; how could I help them?

I reinvented my entire repertoire. The experience broadened my range, and these activities are now part of *ZeroPrep for Beginners*. In "Let's Put on a Play!," Chapter 2, page 28, for example, one student played the part of a cooking pot. He understood a great deal and performed well, though he wasn't ready to speak yet.

A Final Note

The marvelous thing about teaching beginners is that you are the one who takes them on the first step of that very long and exciting journey of new expression and communication. Every time we see a former student, in school or on the job, we are filled with happiness and pride. "I had a part in this! I am part of this student's success!"

Experience has its benefits. Our job has become much easier and more enjoyable over the years, and we want yours to be too. We hope you will enjoy this collection of our all-time favorite activities!

Laurel Pollard	lpollard@u.arizona.edu
Natalie Hess	natalie.hess@nau.edu
Jan Herron	jhsmh2@aol.com

Feedback about this book? More *Zero Prep* ideas? Share them by emailing us!

Chapter One
Listening

It is not easy to listen well in a new language. At first the new language sounds like a noisy stream with no breaks and no logic. Then gradually we recognize a word here and there, then a sentence, then miraculously a whole conversation. Students need plenty of time to practice their listening skills so that these sounds take on meaning, and the activities in this book will help your students do so.

1.1 SINGING DICTATION

People remember songs they learned long ago, even when many other things are forgotten. We can bring the power, and the joy, of song into our classrooms with this simple routine. Even people who think they don't sing enjoy this activity. (Not even the teacher needs to sing well!)

AIM: Listening, pronunciation, spelling, vocabulary expansion

Procedure:

1. Choose a simple melody you and your students know well. Any short tune is fine.

2. Put phrases your students are learning into the melody. For example, if you are using the tune of the "Happy Birthday" song, you might sing,

   > "Good morning to you,
   > Good morning to you!
   > How are you today-ay?
   > I'm glad to see you."

3. Sing the first line. Students sing it back to you chorally. Work on pronunciation of important sounds as you go along.

4. Sing the first and second lines together. Students sing them back.

5. Sing lines 1, 2 and 3. Students sing them back.

6. Sing lines 1, 2, 3 and 4 . Students sing them back.

7. Continue to build up the song in this way.

8. Students write as much as they can remember of the song.

9. Students look at classmates' papers and revise their own.

10. You or a student volunteer writes the song on the board with input from everybody. Final help with grammar and spelling happens here.

11. Students correct what they wrote on their own papers, recopying if necessary.

12. All together, sing the song again.

1.2 USING THE TELEPHONE

Talking on the telephone frightens beginners. This activity will help them gain skills and become more comfortable on the telephone.

AIM : Fluency practice, review

MATERIALS: A bag or envelope for collecting slips of paper.

Procedure:

1. Write a short telephone conversation like the one below on the board. Practice it with the whole class.

   A: Hello, may I speak to _____?

   B: This is _____.

   A: Oh, hello _____. This is _____. Can you meet me for lunch today?

   B: Sure, _____. I'll be glad to. Let's meet at McDonald's at 12 o'clock.

   A: Great! See you then.

   B: Good bye.

   A: Bye!

2. Students write their telephone numbers on pieces of paper.

3. Collect all slips of paper in bag.

4. Students pick a slip of paper—not their own—from bag. (A student who by chance gets his/her own paper, puts it back in the bag.)

5. One student begins by picking up an imaginary phone and holding it to his/her ear. He/she calls out the number on his/her slip, while dialing the number on an imaginary phone. All students must practice active listening.

6. The student who hears his/her number says, "Hello. This is _____." (He/she repeats the number.)

7. The student who has called out the number says "Hello, this is _____." (his/her own name) "May I speak to _____?" (name of student who has answered)

8. These two complete the conversation.

9. The student whose number was called now calls out the number on his/her slip and a new student answers.

10. Continue as long as all students are involved and interested.

Extension: The content of the conversation can, of course, be varied endlessly depending on the level and the ability of the class. For example, you can eliminate certain words and ask students to fill in the blanks. Students can change the time and place. Students can decide that they can't meet.

1.3   LET'S PACK A SUITCASE

Packing a suitcase is fun, and everybody likes to give and receive things. This activity gets students talking! They listen carefully to the directions of others, and then they surprise themselves with how much they can say.

 **AIM:**   Review of clothing, personal items, and color words; fluency practice

Preparation:

1. Photocopy or trace the illustrations, making sure that there is at least one travel item for each member of your class. It is fine for two or three members of the class to have the same travel item, but everyone needs his/her own copy.

2. Cut up the pictures so that you will be able to give a separate travel item to each member of your class.

MATERIALS: Boxes of crayons or color markers (Each student needs about three crayons.)

Procedure:

1. Explain that the class will be going on a trip, and that we have to pack a suitcase. Gesture to create an imaginary suitcase on your desk.

2. Call on a student and give the student the picture of a coat (or any other travel item).

3. Hold up the "coat" saying, "This is the coat we need in our suitcase. Kumiko has the coat." (You may write the word on the board.)

4. Continue this procedure until all the items have been distributed.

5. Call on any student, saying "I need a _____ in my suitcase. Who has a _____?"

6. The student who has the travel item comes up and puts it in the imaginary suitcase. Thank the student profusely and shake his/her hand.

7. Continue until all items are in the suitcase.

8. Volunteers take over your job. One at a time, they come up to the suitcase and give away three items by asking, "Who wants a _____?" They do this until the suitcase is empty.

9. Other volunteers repack the suitcase by saying, "I need a _____ in my suitcase. Who has a _____?"

10. After the items are distributed again, students get crayons and color their items.

11. The above procedure is repeated this time with the addition of the color (for example, "I need a red coat in our suitcase. Who has a red coat?"). Continue packing and unpacking the suitcase as long as students are interested.

Extensions:

1. Follow this same routine by furnishing a house, planting a vegetable garden, or shopping for food for a week.

2. Students write a story called "Planning a good trip to _____." They should include as many items as possible from the list. You can get them started by giving them the opening sentence: "I have always wanted to go to _____. I want it to be a good trip. I need to pack my suitcase carefully. I need _____, and a _____, and a _____." Students create their own closing sentence.

1.4 CATCH THE TEACHER'S MISTAKES

We know the value of being read to. Beginners need a lot of input, and reading aloud can provide many benefits, including intonation, pronunciation, spelling/sound correspondences, and enjoying the new language. So read aloud to your class as they follow along in their textbook. Here's a way to make the routine a little more interesting. It keeps students on their toes and also allows for a bit of role reversal as they correct their teacher's "mistakes."

Here's another benefit: beginners are often shy about asking a speaker to repeat something they didn't understand. In this activity, they must interrupt the speaker. It's a bit easier because they know that the error is not in their listening ability but in what you said. It also helps that everyone in the class is obligated to interrupt you.

AIM: Listening with a specific purpose, interrupting, asking for clarification

MATERIALS: A story from the student text or another source

Procedure:

1. Choose a passage to read aloud to your class.

2. Tell students that sometimes you make mistakes, like everybody else, and that you are going to need their help. If they hear a mistake as you read to them, they should let you know about it! Keep your tone light and amusing.

3. You have options here: Tell students to call out in chorus: "What did you say?" or more simply, "What?" Or tell them to hold up their left hand every time you make a mistake.

4. To demonstrate, say two sentences, one correct and one ridiculous. For example, say, "Ahmed is a good student."

5. Look at the students expectantly. Pause. Then say, "Ahmed is a beautiful woman." They should say, "WHAT?" or put their hands up.

6. Students open their texts. Begin reading aloud. Read the first sentence correctly, but in the second or third sentence make a ridiculous mistake, for example: ". . . so they got into their book and went to the store." (If they don't catch the mistake, raise an eyebrow or repeat the mistake, for example: "Their book? They got into their book?")

7. Continue to read through the story, making an occasional

"mistake" and giving the students the pleasure of interrupting and correcting you.

Extension: In pairs, students choose a paragraph, cross out a few words and write in something ridiculous, then read this to their partner. The partner's job is to interrupt and correct the reader.

1.5 CLASSIC TPR

An Introduction to TPR: The Method

The total physical response method (TPR) was invented by James Asher. It is based on the giving and following of directions. With the TPR method, students learn language very much the same way young children learn their first language. Language learners understand many things before they want to speak, and TPR lets learners use the language through their bodies before they can actually use it for speech. TPR works especially well for beginning learners when the teacher doesn't know the language of the students. Students usually enjoy TPR activities and laugh a lot while they learn. Following are three examples of TPR. You will soon find your own strategies for using this routine. It can be used for any sequential actions such as baking a cake, setting a table, cleaning house, cleaning one's desk, getting ready, or ordering a meal. Be sure that your miming shows the meaning very clearly. Also be sure that every student imitates your actions. Without this physical activity, the words won't mean much or stay in students' memories.

AIM: Listening, following directions, speaking

Procedure:

1. Call four volunteers to come and sit in a row of four chairs facing the class.

2. Sit in the row together with the students. (You are the fifth person.)

3. Say, "Stand up." As you are saying it, stand up. The students will follow your lead. If they don't, motion for them to stand.

4. Say, "Sit down" and sit. Students will also sit.

5. Repeat the procedure several times.

6. Introduce a new word. Say, "Walk" and start walking. Repeat the word, "walk," as you and the four students walk around the room.

7. Say, "Turn around" and turn around as you say it. The students will follow your action.

8. Walk the students back to the chairs and repeat the activity several times, using all the directions you have practiced.

9. Call four new volunteers up to the chairs and repeat the activity.

10. Repeat the procedure with four different volunteers each time until you feel that most of the class is familiar with the words and actions.

11. Repeat the procedure with the entire class.

12. Ask volunteers to call out the actions while other students mime.

1.6 TPR: MAKING TEA

Making and drinking tea is always relaxing. Through this activity, students can relax while they make and drink their imaginary cup of tea.

AIM: Listening, repeating, following directions, speaking, writing

Procedure:

1. Stand in front of the class and say, "I am so thirsty. (Accompany this with some acting; touch your throat to show how parched you are.) "I am going to make myself a nice cup of tea." (Mime drinking tea.)

2. Say the following, and accompany each action with mime:

    I put water in the kettle.
    I put the kettle on the stove.
    I turn on the stove.
    I wait for the water to boil.

While the water is getting hot, I get a cup from the cupboard.
I get a teabag from the box in the cupboard.
I put the teabag in the cup.
Ah, now the water is boiling!
I pour the water into the cup.
I like sugar in my tea, so I get the sugar bowl out of the cupboard, and I put some sugar into my tea.
I also like a slice of lemon in my tea.
So I get a lemon from the refrigerator,
and I slice the lemon.
I put a slice of lemon in my tea.
I take the teabag out and put it on a little plate.
I sit down and I drink the tea. Oh, this is wonderful tea!
How I love a good cup of lemon tea!

3. Call for four volunteers to come to the front of the class. Say, "Now Theresa, Kumiko, Jose, and Wolfgang will make some tea."

4. Say, "First put the water in the kettle." As you say it, demonstrate the action and encourage the volunteers to follow your actions.

5. Go through the entire sequence.

6. Repeat with several groups of volunteers.

7. Repeat with a group without miming the actions for them.

8. Repeat with the entire class.

9. Call for volunteers to give single directions while the class mimes.

10. Call for volunteers to give several directions. Again, the class mimes these.

11. Write the entire list of instructions on the board.

12. Students copy the instructions. Don't worry if it takes quite a bit of time for students to copy the instructions from the board. Students learn the instructions better when they copy them. Also, you can use their papers later, in a review lesson.

13. In pairs, students take turns giving and following the instructions.

14. When you feel that students really know the material, encourage them to add extra steps such as " I like a cookie/some bread with my tea," or "I like honey in my tea," or "I drink tea slowly." (Before making these changes, look at what you have written on the board and together with the class insert new words and phrases.)

15. Eventually students can change tea to coffee and produce new ingredients and steps.

Extension: Here is another set of instructions you can use. Feel free to make up your own!

Say the following, and accompany each action with mime: "I always drive my car to work. This is how I start my car."

> I look for my keys.
> Oh, here are my keys!
> I open the door of the car.
> I get into the car and I shut the door.
> I fasten my seat belt.
> I adjust the car mirrors.
> I release the hand-brake.
> I insert the key.
> I turn the key to start the engine.
> I put the car in "drive."
> I look in the back and side mirrors.
> I turn on the radio to very good music.
> I put my foot on the gas.
> I drive to work.

For further ideas, look at *Action English Pictures* by Noriko Takahashi and Maxine Frauman-Prickel, Alta Book Center Publishers, 1999.

1.7 TPR: MAKING A PEANUT BUTTER SANDWICH

In this variation of TPR, there is more choral repetition. The peanut butter sandwich is an American cultural artifact. We might as well use it for language learning about food.

AIM: Listening, following directions, speaking, writing

MATERIALS: A jar of peanut butter, two slices of bread, and a knife. (If you feel like it, bring enough peanut butter and bread for the whole class.) If you don't have peanut butter, use another food.

Procedure:

1. Stand in front of class and say, "I love peanut butter sandwiches." Hold up the jar and say, "peanut butter."

2. Quickly make yourself a sandwich, take a bite and say, "mmm . . . good." Students will wonder why you are doing this!

3. Say, "How do we make a peanut butter sandwich? Well, . . ." (Tell the steps, miming as you go.)

> First I open the peanut butter jar.
> I get two slices of bread.
> I get some peanut butter from the jar.
> I spread the peanut butter on one slice of bread.
> I put the other slice on top.
> I sit down and eat my sandwich.
> What a good sandwich! I love peanut butter.

4. Call for four volunteers to come to the front of the class. Say, "Now Adam, Deborah, Tamar, and Yuri will make peanut butter sandwiches."

5. Say, "First, I open the jar." As you say it, demonstrate the action. Students repeat your words while they mime opening their own jars.

6. Go through the entire sequence, with the four students repeating your sentences and imitating your actions.

7. Repeat (if necessary) with several groups of volunteers.

8. Go through the instructions again, with the entire class miming and repeating.

9. Say the instructions, this time without miming the actions. Students will look at classmates if they forget what a word means.

10. Write the list of instructions on the board.

11. Students copy the instructions. Circulate, point out where corrections are needed, until everyone has a correct copy. Early finishers can help their classmates.

12. In pairs, students take turns giving and following instructions. One reads, and the listening partner (who *cannot* see the paper) repeats and mimes.

13. A volunteer comes to the front of the class and takes everyone through the instructions. Repeat with other volunteers.

Extension: You may turn this into a party, with peanut butter sandwiches for everyone!

1.8 WHO SAID IT?

Beginning language learners understand much more than they can express in their target language. Here's a task that gives them plenty to read and listen to, then allows them to demonstrate their comprehension with one-word answers.

AIM: Listening comprehension, reading review

MATERIALS: A story from the student text or another source

Procedure:

1. Tell a story or do a reading with your class.

2. Say something that one character said (or might have said). For example, say, "Please let me go to the dance!"

3. Ask the class, "Who said it?"

4. Choose one of the options below:

    1. Volunteers call out the name of the character, for example, "Cinderella!"

    2. Pairs or small groups consult until they reach agreement; then you call on one student from each group to answer.

Variations: With more advanced beginners, teams can make up the things characters would say. They call these out to another team, who must tell who said it. You may set this up as a competitive game.

1.9 STAND FOR YOUR WORD

This activity gives students a feeling that they own certain words and helps them to put these words in context.

AIM: Vocabulary review, reading review

MATERIALS: A text (with questions) that students have read

Procedure:

1. Students take out a piece of paper.

2. Walk around and write one word from the story on each student's paper. The same word may be given to several students.

3. Be sure students know what their words mean. They may get help from other students or from you.

4. Read the text out loud while students listen.

5. As soon as a student hears his/her word, they stand up. Repeat this step a few times if it is challenging for them.

6. Students trade words.

7. Students hold up their new word and call it out. (Again they get help with meaning, if necessary.)

8. Read the text aloud again while students stand up each time they hear their new word.

9. Repeat steps 6-8 several times.

10. Write the words on the board in the order that they appeared in the text.

11. Students look at the text and read out the sentences where "their words" appeared.

12. Students read the whole text and answer the questions.

1.10 NOISY TRUE/FALSE

Even though this activity has a lot of moving around, it is a good assessment of students' recall of a previously read text, as well as their listening skills.

AIM: Listening for statements that are true or false

MATERIALS: A story that the students have just read

Procedure:

1. Write TRUE on the board on one side of the room.
2. Write FALSE on the board on the other side of the room.
3. Somewhere between the two, write PLEASE REPEAT THE SENTENCE.
4. All students stand in the middle of the room.
5. Say, "I am going to read sentences from the story we just finished. Some sentences will be true and some will be false. If the sentence is true, run and stand under the word TRUE. If it is false, run and stand under the word FALSE. If you aren't sure, stand under the PLEASE REPEAT sign."
6. Read sentences from the text, changing some words to make false statements.
7. Stop after each sentence as students run and stand where they want to be.
8. If anyone is standing under the PLEASE REPEAT sign, read the sentence again until they move to the TRUE or FALSE sign.
9. Discussion and argument can follow.
10. Read the correct sentence to show which group is correct.
11. Students move back to the middle of the room to hear the next statement and choose their positions.
12. Repeat until you have finished the text.

Note: Encourage students to think for themselves, not just follow the crowd. Tell them to stand up for what they believe is correct, even if they are standing alone!

1.11 SILENT TRUE/FALSE

Quiet or shy students who are easily overwhelmed by the loud, vocal ones can excel at this activity.

AIM: Listening for statements that are true or false

MATERIALS: Something to read to the students and two 3" x 5" cards or pieces of paper for each student.

Procedure:

1. Students listen as you read the text several times.
2. Give each student two cards.
3. Students write TRUE on one card and FALSE on the other.
4. Say, "I will read sentences from the text. Some will be true, and some will be false. If the sentence is true, hold up the TRUE card, if it's false, hold up the FALSE card."
5. Read sentences from the text. Change some words to make some false statements.
6. Everyone must be silent each time you speak a sentence until all cards are held up; then discussion can follow.
7. Read the exact sentence from the text for students to hear the correct answer.
8. Give all students the text to read at home or in class.

1.12 PICTURE DICTATION

Students have such fun drawing that they may not notice how much they are learning! They use visual and spoken information to create a picture and recreate sentences. You can use this activity to teach or review vocabulary, and it's a wonderful way to practice prepositions of location.

AIM: Speaking, listening, vocabulary

Procedure:

1. Dictate an imaginary "picture" to your class. Adjust the dictation to your students' level. For example, in a low beginners' class, dictate a few nouns and see whether students can draw them. You can also review vocabulary and structures they've already studied by making up a paragraph like the one on the next page.

In the middle of the picture there is a house.
In front of the house there is a tree.
Above the house there is an airplane.
To the left of the house there is a happy girl.

2. Students listen to the description.

3. Dictate again while the students draw the picture.

4. In pairs, students look at their completed pictures. They notice similarities and differences and talk about what they drew.

5. A volunteer goes to the board. The class tells him/her what to draw to recreate the picture on the board. (Help with their language if necessary.)

6. Go to the big picture on the board and point to the house. Students say: "In the middle of the picture there is a house." Write this sentence by the house. Continue until everything in the picture has a sentence by it. (You may have some students advanced enough to write the sentences on the board themselves!)

1.13 I CHALLENGE!

This is a good speaking and listening follow-up after students have written something. Often students can hear mistakes that they can't find when they silently read their own writing. This routine leads to vigorous group discussions as challengers are themselves challenged by other students. In addition to exploring what's right and wrong, this is one of the best activities we know for focused listening. Use it often!

AIM: Student correction of writing errors, reading aloud, listening

MATERIALS: Students' writing

Procedure:

1. Ask who in the class thinks that they did a pretty good job on their writing. Usually someone will volunteer (maybe with a little encouragement).

2. Tell the class that this good volunteer will begin to read from their paper, but the listeners have a big job—to listen for mistakes.

3. If someone hears what they consider to be a mistake, they jump up and yell, "I challenge!"

4. They state the mistake and their correction.

5. The whole class discusses the alleged mistake and the proposed correction. The teacher is the supreme judge who settles all disputes.

6. If the challenger is correct, she/he gets to start reading from their paper until they are challenged.

7. If the original reader is correct, they continue reading until another challenge arises, or until they finish.

8. The whole thing starts over again with a new reader.

Notes:

1. *If classmates are too shy to challenge at first, you can encourage them with exaggerated looks of shock or disbelief when you hear a mistake that is unchallenged. Also, look carefully at the students. Sometimes a student's face will show if they hear an error, even if they don't speak up. With a little encouragement, they will join in.*

2. *Use this activity after your students have gotten acquainted and trust each other.*

1.14 BINGO

Bingo helps students make repeated sight-sound associations. You may use:

- Alphabet letters or the numbers 1 through 9
- Numbers that tend to confuse (50/15, for example)
- Money amounts ($3.15, $1.75)

 **AIM:** Spelling, listening, pronunciation

Procedure:

1. Dictate a list of letters, numbers, or words. After students write down each item, write the list on the board so they can check their spelling.

2. Draw a 9- or 16-square grid on the board.

3. Students copy the grid onto their own paper, putting the items in random order. Show them that they must put each item in different squares. Every student's paper will have the words in different places.

4. Call out the items one at a time. As students find the item in their grid, they cross it off.

5. As soon as a student has a vertical, horizontal, or diagonal straight line of crossed-out items, the student calls out, "Bingo."

6. This student dictates the items in his/her straight line as you stand nearby and everyone listens. If the student pronounces the items correctly, she/he is the winner of this round! Classmates can help with mistakes.

7. Play it again, for as long as students are challenged and enjoying themselves.

Variation: Use vocabulary words that can be demonstrated (action verbs, body parts, real objects). Just mime the action or point to the object instead of dictating the word.

1.15 GOSSIP

This activity often leads to funny results while giving students quick feedback about their pronunciation and an immediate chance to do better.

AIM: Pronunciation, listening

Procedure:

1. Arrange students in a circle or a line.

2. Say something quietly into the ear of the first student. You can use any vocabulary or grammar you have been working with, but it should be short. For example, "I found $100 yesterday."

3. The student murmurs what you said to the next person, who passes it on. (If other students can overhear as the message is passed along, teach everyone to hum—perhaps with fingers in ears—until their turns come.)

4. The last student tells the entire class what he or she thought the message was. The result is usually hilarious.

5. Where did the changes come from? All students tell what they thought they heard. This provides speakers with useful feedback about their pronunciation.

6. Do another round immediately, encouraging everyone to speak as clearly as possible.

Note: Eight to ten students is best. If your group is large, demonstrate with eight to ten students, then form groups to play the game.

Chapter Two
Speaking

Speaking gives you power. When you can't say what you want to say, you literally feel "dumb" in all the meanings of this word. When people first learn a new language, they want to say something and they want to say it right. They want to smile and add the word *thank you* or *please* to their smiles. They want to be able to do all those things that their mouths have helped them with in their own language. These activities will help students to get a lot of practice in being themselves through their own voices in a new language, and you can join them in the fun and the discovery.

2.1 WHAT'S YOUR NAME? NICE TO MEET YOU

This activity is a way to give students the polite phrases they need on their first day of class.

 **AIM:** Introductions

Procedure:

1. Stand and say to your class. "My name is _____."
   (Give your first name or the name you want your students to
   call you.) Write your name on the board.

2. Repeat this very clearly so that students understand what you
   are saying.

3. Repeat several times.

4. Point to a student and say, "What's your name?"

5. The student responds with, "My name is Sarah." (Help as
   needed.)

6. Go to that student and shake hands, saying, " Nice to meet
   you, Sarah."

7. Repeat with several students, until the idea is clear.

8. On the board, write:

   My name is _____.
   What is your name?
   Nice to meet you.

9. Students stand. Demonstrate how they should move around
   asking one another for names, shaking hands and responding
   with, "Nice to meet you."

10. Students continue to mingle as long as interest is high.

2.2 PLEASE AND THANK YOU

Beginners in a language need to know polite words right away. This
is a good way to get them started.

 **AIM:** Teaching *please* and *thank you*

Procedure:

1. Teach the words *book, pencil,* and *paper.*

2. On the board write:

> Can I please have your book (pencil, paper)?
> Thank you.

3. Students stand, each holding a book, a pencil and a piece of paper.

4. Go up to a student and ask, "Can I please have your book?" while gesturing appropriately.

5. When you get the book, say, "Thank you."

6. Repeat the procedure with several students, each time asking for something different.

7. Do a choral reading with the whole class with the phrases you have written on the board.

8. Students mingle, acting out the *please/thank you* scenario.

9. Continue as long as interest is high.

10. Tell the class, "Please sit down." When they do, say, "Thank you!"

2.3 TAKING SURVEYS

This speaking activity helps students to get to know one another. It generates a lot of useful words because the content comes from students' own lives.

 **AIM:**   Fluency practice

Procedure:

1. Draw the following table on the board.

Name of Student	Favorite Food	Favorite Color	Favorite Place	Favorite Person	Favorite Activity

2. Students copy it, listing all their classmates' names in the first column.

3. Explain any unknown words in the chart.

4. Students practice the following question both chorally and individually: "What is your favorite _____?" (Practice this for each category.)

5. Students mingle to interview classmates. They should ask each partner only one question, write that one answer, and then move on to another student. The idea is to mingle. They may, however, return to a student several times.

6. Circulate, helping out with vocabulary and encouraging students to ask the complete question.

7. Continue as long as interest is high. The charts need not be completely filled.

8. Students return to their seats with their charts. Ask, "Who knows what Alia's favorite activity is?"

9. Volunteers answer. Write useful words on the board as they come up. Students listen carefully so they can put these words in their own charts.

Extension: The same routine can be used to review any material by changing the categories on the chart.

2.4   CARRY THE MESSAGE

This versatile routine is useful with almost any content. The description below explains how to use it for practicing question formation, but variations are also listed.

We often ask our students questions, for example, when we review a reading. When students repeat our questions, there are two good results:

• They improve their command of question formation.

• The repetitions lead them to a more thorough understanding of the text.

 **AIM:** Question formation, reviewing a reading

Procedure:

1. Put students in groups of three. One student is A, one is B, and one is C.

2. Ask a question. It is more authentic if the C's don't hear the question from you. Here are three ways to do this:

   • Have the C's turn their backs while you write the question on the board for the A's and B's.

   • Have the C's put their fingers in their ears and hum while you tell the question to A's and B's.

   • If your group is not large, invite the A's and B's to come up and cluster around you to hear the question, then go back to tell it to their C partners.

3. In each group, A and B repeat your question to C.

4. C answers the question.

5. For the next question, you may keep students in the same role or tell them to rotate jobs within their trio so that a different student will answer.

Variations: Use this routine with things other than questions. For example:

1. To review a reading, tell A and B a vocabulary word; C must find a sentence in the reading where that word appears. This works very well with low beginners. Use it in the first week of class, then build up, so that students are carrying whole-sentence messages later in your course.

2. Give A and B an answer. C provides the question.

3. Give A and B a color. C tells the names of some things in the room that are that color.

4. Give A and B a category like "Things we eat." C has to tell the names of some foods.

5. Use your imagination! This routine is useful for almost any topic. You can even add a writing component to C's job, if you wish.

2.5 CLASSROOM LANGUAGE

When you put up some helpful phrases in your classroom right at the beginning of a course, students feel taken care of. They know that help is there if they need it. This is especially important for beginners, who may be living in an ongoing panic of "I don't understand" without even knowing how to tell you. Having easy access to important classroom phrases in the first week makes everyone more comfortable, which helps them learn more easily.

AIM: Fostering independence in the classroom

PREPARATION: Make signs, with one of the classroom phrases below on each sign. These must be large enough to read at a distance. They should be colorful. Illustrate them, if possible.

MATERIALS: Blank paper for making signs, colored markers (if available)

Procedure:

1. Notice those sentences or phrases that your students need to say each day.

2. On the first or second day with a new group, bring in the signs.

    Classroom Phrases
    What does _____ mean?
    I don't understand.
    How do you spell _____?
    How do you say _____?
    Help me, please.

3. Post these where everyone can see them. Explain/demonstrate the meanings of these phrases. Tell students that they can use these signs for help in class. For example, say "How do you spell 'cat'?" "You spell 'cat' C - A - T." (Write this on the board.)

4. Whenever someone struggles to say one of these phrases (or says it in their native language) just smile and point to the sign. The student then says it in English.

5. As time goes on, encourage students to use the phrase correctly during classwork *without* looking at the sign. Ask them, "Can I take this down now?" If they say, "No!" tell them, "OK, we'll take it down later."

6. When you see that they aren't using that sign any more, make a celebration out of taking it down. "We've learned this!" Later, when you point to the empty spot and say "What was this?" They will know!

Optional: Add new signs as part of your ongoing lessons, if this is appropriate. For example:

2.6 READING AND SPEAKING 3 X 3

Try this routine once, and the whole class will be hooked! This is great for beginners because it involves repeatedly reading and telling the same story—something they always need.

 AIM: Reading comprehension, speaking in sentences, listening, confidence building

MATERIALS: Two stories from the students' textbook or another source

Procedure:

1. Divide the class into two equal groups.
2. Give members of group 1 the same story to read to themselves.
3. Give members of group 2 another story to read to themselves.
4. Students read their stories to themselves three times.
5. While they are reading, circulate and help with vocabulary and comprehension.
6. While they are reading, write key words from each story on the board. Choose words you see they are having some difficulty with.
7. After they have read the story three times, have students turn the story over so they can't see it and tell the story to a

partner from their same group. They will tell it three times to this partner and then that same partner will tell it to them three times. This is to prepare for telling the story to a partner who hasn't read it.

8. Make new partners with a member from group 1 and a member from group 2.

9. The new partners tell their stories to each other three times each.

10. Walk around and give "speaking grades" if you need to, or write down grammar problems to be discussed later.

11. Give all the students the story they did not read, and give them time to read the stories.

12. Discuss the stories together or ask comprehension questions.

Note:

- *It is strongly suggested that you do this routine often, with different stories. The first time the students try this, they find it extremely difficult, but by the end of several weeks, they are much more at ease and can happily see their progress.*

- *If your students are low beginners, you may have many key words on the board—perhaps most of the story. That's okay. The subsequent times you do this, you can write fewer and fewer words, until at the end of the term the students need no helping words—another thing that makes them happy about their progress!*

2.7   LET'S PUT ON A PLAY!

Learners who read for a specific purpose—and the more fun the better—are much more motivated to understand than those who read just to answer questions or take a test. *Important: Don't tell the students that this will be a play. They are much more at ease and ready for fun if they find this out after they know the story.* Once students have done a story as a play, they never forget it. They have so much fun that they don't even realize how much they're learning! And it's surprisingly easy to do!

AIM: Reading improvement, speaking

MATERIALS: A story from the textbook or another source, blank paper for drawing pictures, colored markers, tape

Procedure:

1. Read the story to the class, several times if necessary.
2. Ask a few questions and talk about the story to check comprehension.
3. Give each student a copy of the story.
4. They read the story silently.
5. Help with vocabulary as needed.
6. In pairs, students read the story aloud to each other. (There are several good ways to do this: each may read the entire story, they may alternate paragraphs, or they may alternate sentences.)
7. Tell the class that they are going to perform this story as a play. They need not memorize. They can read their parts during the play.
8. The class decides what roles and characters are needed. If there are not enough speaking parts, use students for other parts, like a door that opens, a chair, etc. Students may volunteer, or you may assign the parts. You will need several narrators.
9. Optional: Together with the students, make props. Usually pictures drawn on paper are good enough.
10. Each student writes his/her role or character name on a piece of paper, for example: Goldilocks, Mama Bear, Papa's chair, etc.
11. Students tape their signs on their chests. Everyone is now "labeled."
12. Practice, practice, practice. Go through the story, coaching students as needed. Do this as many times as necessary, until students are comfortable with their parts.
13. Perform the play. This is usually such a big hilarious mess that the students like to do it two or three times. An audience is nice also—maybe another class, office staff, anyone walking in the hall, etc.

14. Discuss how the play went, what students liked, and what they would change. Talk about plays in general. For example, what is the director's job (that's you), why are props important, etc.

15. Students reread the story silently. (This could be homework.)

16. Ask comprehension questions about the story.

Extensions:

1. Choose two or three stories, depending on the size of your class.

2. Assign a group of students to each story.

3. Step up into the role of producer. Tell students that you will provide the stories, and they'll take over from there.

4. Each group selects one student as director and assigns roles.

5. Following the steps above, students produce plays and perform for the other groups.

2.8   CORRECTING PAPERS I: SEEK AND FIND

> ### A Note on Correcting Papers
>
> Correcting a set of student papers one by one is not the most valuable use of a teacher's time. These three activities will free you for more important work while giving your students immediate feedback on their work.
>
> When you want to know how individual students did, encourage students not to erase and change their incorrect answers during the activity, but rather to circle their errors and write the corrections above the circle. Collect the papers and use them as your guide in planning your next lessons.

In this activity, students first hear the correction, then see it on a classmate's paper.

 **AIM:**   Correcting student papers, speaking (polite disagreement), learning from classmates

Procedure:

1. Read out the correct answers.
2. Students check their own papers, circling but not correcting words they got wrong.
3. Everyone stands and mingles, looking for papers that have correct answers to those items.
4. When they find a classmate who does not have that word circled, they copy the correct answer on their own paper.
5. Students circulate until they have found and copied all the corrections for the circles on their paper.

2.9 CORRECTING PAPERS II: PAPER SWAP

Students can often find errors on a classmate's paper that they would miss on their own.

This highly visual activity is excellent for guiding students toward what they need to study at home. When students see many circles, they are motivated to study more!

AIM: Correcting student papers, speaking (polite disagreement), learning from classmates

MATERIALS: The correct answers to an assignment, one copy for each student (If you don't have handouts, you can write the correct answers on the board, then erase them before step 4.)

Procedure:

1. Students exchange papers.
2. Give answer keys to students.
3. Students circle but do not correct the errors on their classmate's paper.
4. Collect the answer keys or erase the board.
5. Students take their own papers back. You have options here:
   - Students correct their own papers, now that their errors have been located.
   - Students work on corrections in pairs or trios.

Variation: Leave the answer keys with students so they can correct their own papers in class or at home. (This is wonderful for spelling!)

2.10 CORRECTING PAPERS III: PAPER PAIRS

In this activity, you do not give the correct answers at first. Students discuss and debate whose answer is correct. Use this when students are near mastery of an assignment.

AIM: Correcting student papers, speaking (polite disagreement), learning from classmates

Procedure:

1. In pairs, students compare their papers.
2. They discuss the differences they find and decide who is correct.
3. If they can't agree, they may visit other pairs for help and/or ask you for help.
4. Give the correct answers so students can confirm that their decisions were correct.

2.11 CONCENTRIC CIRCLE TALK

This requires a precursor activity that ensures that the students know enough vocabulary. This could be a reading activity, sentence expansion, or even a "what did you do last weekend" chain. This fluency activity is a great confidence builder. Students learn to add information as they rotate around to partner after partner. They are surprised by how much language they can produce!

AIM: Fluency

Procedure:

1. Walk around the room, counting off students: "One, two, one, two . . ." etc., until everyone knows their number.
2. All "ones" stand up.
3. Help these students stand in a circle, facing inward.
4. Stand with them in the circle. Tell them, "Turn around so you're facing out." Demonstrate this.
5. All "twos" stand up.
6. Each "two" stands across from a partner in the circle.
7. Tell the inner circle students, "Your job is to listen."

8. Tell the outer circle students, "Your job is to speak. You will speak for thirty seconds. Tell your partner as much as you can. Go!"

9. Time them. After 30 seconds, stop the speakers.

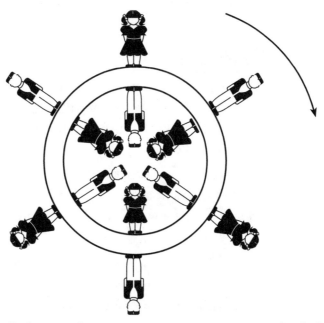

10. Tell the speakers to move one position to the left, and demonstrate this. All speakers now have a new listener.

11. They tell the same story (or information), this time speaking for one full minute.

12. Again, speakers move one place to their left.

13. Speakers talk to their third partner, again on the same topic, for one or two minutes.

14. Speakers and listeners change places. Students who were inner-circle listeners are now outer-circle speakers. Repeat steps 8 through 13.

Extension: After everyone sits, ask (for example), "Who heard Jose's story?" Three students raise their hands. Ask each student to tell you one thing they remember, starting with the quietest student, just to give him/her a chance. Continue as long as interest is high.

Variation: If the content is a reading that students have done, and if they had some difficulty with step 9, let the speakers run back to their desks for a quick rereading before they rotate to a new partner. They'll have more to say! You can let speakers scan the reading quickly at each stage of the game, if you wish.

2.12 POINTING-OUT FUN

Students laugh a lot in this activity. For once, it is correct to be incorrect!

AIM: Vocabulary review, practicing simple affirmative and negative sentences, practicing *this* vs. *that* (see extension)

Procedure:

1. Review objects in the room, including students' clothing and parts of the body, by walking around the room and saying things like, "This is a window." Students repeat these statements chorally.

2. Bring two students up to demonstrate the activity. They both stand near a window (for example). One says to the other, "This is a window." The listener responds, "Yes, this is a window."

3. They do this with a few objects.

4. Students pair up and walk around pointing out objects and using the two sentences. Continue this for a few minutes.

5. Students sit down.

6. Do the activity again, this time with negatives. This is where it really becomes fun! Stand near the window again with a student. Point to it and say, "This is a door."

7. Prompt the student to respond, "No, this is not a door! This is a window!" The class chorally repeats both sentences.

8. Do a few more examples. Each time, be sure to stand near the object.

9. Students pair up and walk around, pointing to something and saying that it is something else.

10. Continue as long as students are having fun.

Variation: For low beginners, put these two sentences on the board:

> This is a _____.
> Yes, this is a _____.

Later, add this sentence to the board:

> No, this is not a _____. This is a _____.

Students may refer to these as they work. When students hesitate or make a mistake, just point to the board! Ask students when you may erase the sentences.

Extensions:

1. Students switch partners and go around the room again. (They can switch several times.)
2. With more advanced beginners, stand farther from the object sometimes so you can contrast *that* and *this*. "*This* is a window. *That* is a door."

Chapter Three
Reading

The minute we know how to read, all the books in the world are really open to us, and we can see the thoughts of people far away and know of places where we have never been. Reading in another language is a difficult and technical skill that demands patience and much practice. But when our students learn how to read, they meet those new words again and again, and their language skills improve dramatically. When we help our students to find pleasure in reading, we are helping them to build their new language into something lasting and powerful. The reading activities in this book will help us to do that without the burden of over-preparation.

3.1 ON THE WALL OUTSIDE

Running and drawing in English class? Why not! No one gets sleepy when you use this wonderful activity.

AIM: Speaking clearly, listening for information

MATERIALS: A short list of sentences that describe something students can draw (Make one copy for every pair of students. Words in big type work best.)

Make your own list of sentences to deal with vocabulary or grammar that you have been practicing. Here's a typical example:

> I see a table.
> A small dog is under the table.
> A bird is over the table.
> A big cat is on the table.

Procedure:

1. Post the descriptions on the wall outside the classroom.
2. Put students in pairs: a "speaker" and a "drawer."
3. Each "drawer" sits at a desk with a clean piece of paper, ready to draw.
4. Speakers go outside and read the first sentence.
5. They hurry back in to their partners and tell them what to draw. (It's best if they keep their hands behind their backs and rely on words to do the job!)
6. They continue going back and forth until they've completed their drawings.
7. As each pair finishes, they continue with the last two steps.
8. Pairs compare their pictures with other pairs, discussing the similarities and differences in their drawings.
9. Speakers go outside and bring back a copy of the list of sentences. Partners take turns reading the sentences to each other as they look at their drawing.

You may want to follow this with "Listening Dictacomp," Chapter 4, page 48 (so this "input" language is used as "output" by students).

Acknowledgment: This is an adaptation of an activity we learned from Kevin Keating at the University of Arizona's Center for English as a Second Language.

3.2 WHAT'S THE STORY?

This activity uses all four skills. Students not only remember what they read, but also think about how to retell it. To reinforce what they have learned, they re-create it one more time by writing it.

AIM: Reading practice, summary practice

MATERIALS: A short reading passage from the student's textbook or another source

Procedure:

1. Choose any short reading passage.
2. Read the first line of a passage or read until the end of the first sentence.
3. Students repeat chorally.
4. Students repeat individually.
5. Say, "Choose a word!" (Sometimes you will make a more specific suggestion, such as "What's the action?" "Where did this happen?" "Who did it?")
6. Students call out words.
7. Choose a key word and write it on the board.
8. Continue this process for each sentence until you've reached the end of the reading passage.
9. In pairs, students read the passage to each other.
10. Without looking at the reading, volunteers retell the passage by looking only at the important words on the board.
11. Students write the passage by just following the words on the board. (Even if they only get a few words right, this is good practice!)
12. Students compare their written passage with the original text.

3.3   THE TRUE AND FALSE WAY OF READING

This activity promotes accurate reading and helps students to teach one another.

It's a wonderful activity to do before a test because students learn the meaning of *true* and *false*. It also helps students look closely at the details of a text.

 **AIM:**   Reading for details

Procedure:

1. Tell students four to six sentences, some true and some obviously false. Students tell you which are true and which are false. Examples:

    "Tomas is a woman."
    "Natalia is a woman."
    "My pen is blue." (Hold up a red pen.)
    "You are learning English."
    "Dogs talk."
    "All Americans are rich."

2. Write on the board a sentence from a recently read passage. For example, "Mr. Jenkins owns a store."

3. Ask, "Is this true?" Students say, "Yes."

4. Ask, "How can we make this false?"

5. Volunteers offer ideas. They may change the name, the verb, or another detail.

6. Put students in groups of three.

7. Assign a few sentences from the reading passage to each group.

8. In each group, students take turns reading one sentence each.

9. In the same groups, students write a few true/false statements.

10. Circulate, helping with vocabulary.

11. Each group joins another group, making groups of six.

12. They quiz each other, using the true/false statements they have written.

13. The listening group changes each false statement back to a true one. For example, if a student reads, "Mr. Jenkins owns a horse," a listening student says, "That's false! Mr. Jenkins owns a store."

3.4 POPCORN READING

This read-and-repeat activity makes students pay very close attention to what is being read. It's exciting because students never know when a classmate will call on them to take the next turn.

AIM: Recalling and recreating a reading passage

MATERIALS: A copy of a short reading text (or a list of sentences) for each student

Procedure:

1. Read the text aloud, sentence by sentence.
2. Students repeat each sentence chorally, then individually.
3. When the passage has been read through, assign a class reader (Junko, for example) who stands and rereads the first sentence.
4. Junko chooses another student, saying, for example, "Maxim, please repeat." Junko sits down.
5. Maxim stands and repeats the sentence without looking at the text.
6. Maxim chooses a classmate to read the next sentence, saying, for example, "Maria, please read the next sentence." Maxim sits down.
7. Maria stands up and reads sentence number two, then chooses a classmate to repeat it.
8. Continue until the reading is finished.

3.5 WORDS AND DEFINITIONS

Students really concentrate in this lively pre-reading activity. Repetition becomes interesting and students read the passage thoroughly as they learn new words.

AIM: Pre-reading, vocabulary development

PREPARATION: Prepare three questions on a passage that will be read in class.

Procedure:

1. Students read the passage silently, putting circles around all the words they don't know.

2. Students write these unknown words on the board. One word may appear many times.

3. Explain all new words, eliciting help from students.

4. Don't skip repeated words; review them. These are the words that most students are just learning.

5. Choose seven to ten of the most useful words and ask students' help in writing meanings or synonyms. This may provide opportunities to teach related words. For example, if the target word is *thief* and a student says, "He takes money," teach the verb *steal*.

6. Write each definition on a single piece of paper. For example, write: "A person who steals."

7. Hold up the definition paper. Volunteers call out the word.

8. Repeat this for all the words, holding up definition after definition.

9. Call students' attention to the board where the words are still written, and ask, "Who can find the word that means _____?"

10. Volunteers answer, calling out the word that matches your definition.

11. Students return to the text and find the sentences where these words were used.

12. Volunteers read these sentences.

13. Ask a few comprehension questions. You may call on individuals or let students work in groups.

14. Point to each word while volunteers give you the definitions. This allows more advanced students to shine while others get an extra review.

3.6 ADD A PICTURE

Students learn to recall the action in a story by drawing. This activity works very well in multilevel classes because students can produce many drawings or just a few.

AIM: Becoming familiar with recalling and telling a story, putting events in sequence, speaking, listening

MATERIALS: At least two stories with action from the students' textbooks or other source (fables and simple folktales work well).
Small pieces of paper (four or five inches on a side). You will need enough for each pair of students to have eight or nine pieces.

Procedure:

1. In pairs, students read a story. (Different pairs may have a different story or the same one.)

2. Pairs read their stories several times, first silently, then aloud to each other if they wish.

3. Circulate and help where needed.

4. All students put their stories away.

5. Give each pair two pieces of paper.

6. Tell the students to draw what happened first in the story on one paper, and what happened last in the story on the other paper. These are to be sketches, not particularly good drawings!

7. As students finish the two drawings, give each pair another piece of paper to draw something that happened in the middle of the story.

8. Each pair puts the three papers on a desk, with spaces between them, in a horizontal line, facing the pair.

9. Go around and add two blank papers to each pair's drawings, one between the first and middle, and one between the middle and end.

10. Ask, "What happened here . . . and here?"

11. Students draw more pictures. If students need to, they may briefly look at the story. (Then they must put the story away again.)

12. Go around adding paper squares wherever there is a gap in a student's story until all pairs have a long string of pictures that illustrate their story.

13. As students finish, they tell their story to another pair who has a different story and show each other their pictures. (If every pair reads the same story, this still works well because they will have drawn different pictures and chosen different incidents.)

Extensions:

1. To add writing to the activity, students may add a one-sentence caption to each picture.

2. Post the stories and pictures around the room for all students to see and admire.

3. Ask the listeners questions about the stories. For example, "Who told the story about a fox?" or "Where does the farmer live?"

Note: If a pair insists that they absolutely cannot draw, you have options:

- *Let each of them become the third person in a drawing pair.*

- *Ask the non-drawing pair to just write a phrase for each event.*

3.7 PREDICTING FROM THE TITLE

Rather than telling students about what they're going to read, just jump right into a reading and let the students tell you! These two activities train students in the skill of guessing.

AIM: Pre-reading

MATERIALS: A reading

Procedure:

1. Call students' attention to the title. You may read it, write it on the board, or have a student read it.

2. In small groups, students talk about what they think this reading might be about.

3. Groups report their ideas to the whole class. Note some of these on the board.

4. Students read the article or story.

5. In plenary, discuss how close their predictions were.

3.8 PREDICTING FROM THE PICTURE

Reading is a continual process of predicting and confirming predictions. Even beginners can learn to read effectively; this activity helps students develop the habit of active reading.

AIM: Pre-reading

MATERIALS: A picture that goes with a reading (You may draw it yourself!)

Procedure:

1. Call students' attention to the picture. Elicit words and phrases; talk about what is in the picture.

2. Tell the students that this picture goes with a reading.

3. Ask what they think the reading might be about; write their ideas on the board.

4. Read the passage aloud as students look at their own copies of the passage.

5. Stop occasionally to look at the board. Mark correct predictions with a check, draw a line through incorrect predictions or erase them. Put a question mark next to the predictions students aren't sure about yet.

6. Students reread the passage silently.

7. In pairs, students take turns reading the sentences on the board to each other.

3.9 FINGER SKIM

This low-pressure activity shows students that they don't need to understand every word they read.

AIM: Pre-reading

MATERIALS: A reading passage presented in narrow, not wide columns

Procedure:

1. Demonstrate "finger drag" to carry eyes down the center of the reading by holding your book up for all to see, putting your finger in the middle of the first line of text, and moving your finger straight down, slowly but without stopping, to the bottom of the text.

2. Tell students, "I didn't look at all the words. I looked only at the middle of the reading. My eyes followed my finger. But I can remember some things!" Tell them a few words you saw. Keep this very simple, so they don't feel pressured by your example.

3. Students open their books to a different reading.

4. When you call, "Begin!" students do a "finger drag" down the new reading. Call "Stop!" several seconds later.

5. With books closed, students call out as many words as they can remember. Write these on the board and collectively reconstruct some of the ideas in the reading.

Note: If students are collectively getting about half the meaning, you have found the right difficulty level. If not, make it easier next time by:

- *using an easier passage*
- *having them "finger drag" twice, once on the left and once on the right side of the reading*
- *giving them a little more time for the finger drag.*

Acknowledgment: We learned this activity from Laurel's sister Darcie Smith, a creative elementary school teacher in Nevada.

Chapter Four
Writing

Writing is the most difficult of all the four skills, but when beginning language learners write something down, they have added a physical element to their acquisition process. Shaping the letters and putting words into sentences gives us just one more way of knowing and making something our own. Writing will help our students to organize their thinking and it will move them in the direction of becoming more complete persons in the new language.

4.1 LISTENING DICTACOMP

An Introduction to Dictacomps

The "dictacomp" is a combination of two techniques, dictation and composition. It is an excellent way to teach paraphrasing. A highly adaptable routine, dictacomp can also be used for pre-reading, reviewing material, recycling vocabulary, and reinforcing a grammar point. The great advantage of a dictacomp is that it provides instant feedback.

Dictacomps are adaptable. Depending on your purposes, students may try to reconstruct the original precisely, or they may paraphrase, using prompts to recreate meaning in their words.

This activity is one of the classic routines. You can use it again and again. It helps students become aware of the connecting words in English; it's also a great way to recycle a reading passage to reinforce vocabulary and grammar.

This is good to do after "Reporter/Writer," Chapter 4, page 51.

AIM: Writing, listening

MATERIALS: A previously read passage

Procedure:

1. Choose any short passage your class has previously read. This may be a single sentence or a few short sentences. (A humorous passage works great!)

2. Put key words on the board. Review their meaning and pronunciation.

3. Read the passage slowly while students listen. (They are not looking at the passage, only at the key words. They are not writing.)

4. Read the passage again while students write as much as they can. Read it as many times as the students want you to.

5. In small groups, students rewrite the passage, trying to get it as

close to the original as possible. (Each group produces one paper.)

6. A representative of each group reads the group's paper to the whole class. As each group reads, other groups contribute corrections and/or additions.

7. Read the original passage aloud to the class again.

8. Students look at the original passage to complete and correct their group paper.

Extension: Volunteers tell the passage to the whole class or to a partner.

4.2   WHERE IS THE MISTAKE?

This confidence-building exercise works well as a concentration routine and a settling-down activity. It promotes written accuracy and also serves as a good review of content.

 **AIM:**   Error correction, review of a reading

Procedure:

1. Take several sentences from a text students have just read and write them up on the board, creating obvious errors as you write them. For example: spelling mistakes, punctuation and capitalization mistakes, and grammar mistakes (wrong tense or leaving off the 's' on third person singular).

2. Volunteers come to the front and underline the mistakes.

3. The class as a whole offers suggestions for corrections.

4. Students open their books and check their corrections.

4.3 LET'S CORRECT THOSE MISTAKES!

After students have written something, teach them to read over their papers before they turn them in. Start this habit early in your course! Use this activity immediately after students finish writing. Make corrections as a whole class, not singling out or naming individuals.

AIM: Proofreading, group sentence correction, individual sentence correction

MATERIALS: Students' writing

Procedure:

1. Quickly scan the papers and choose some incorrect sentences.
2. Write one incorrect sentence on the board. For example: "Gloria eat everyday a hamburger."
3. Tell the class that there are mistakes in this sentence.
4. Ask, "Can anyone find them?"
5. Write on the board the correction that someone yells out, and have a class discussion to see if indeed it is a correction. If it is correct, discuss why. For example, say, "Why do we need an 's' on *eat?*"
6. Work on corrections as long as there are mistakes and the class seems interested. You have options here:
   - You may leave the corrected sentences on the board.
   - If your students are a bit more advanced, erase the sentences.
7. Return the papers to their writers. Say, "Now look at your own papers. Do you have the third person singular 's' on your verbs?" (Name a few other errors you've just worked on.)
8. Let the students proofread carefully for mistakes, correct the mistakes, and turn in the papers again.

4.4 REPORTER/WRITER

In this lively dictation activity, students run back and forth reading from a paragraph on the wall. There is a genuine need for students to pronounce as well as they can; their writing partner will insist on it because he/she can't write it unless he/she understands what the reporter said.

AIM: Reinforcing vocabulary, stressing grammar points, speaking clearly, listening

MATERIALS: A short, simple paragraph from students' textbook or another source (several copies for a large class) Consider the following:

- Use a paragraph (or a few short sentences, for low beginners) targeting the grammar or vocabulary you've been studying.
- Use one paragraph from a reading to preview what students will read.
- Use a paragraph they've already read and studied.

Procedure:

1. Post copies of the paragraph on the wall or in the hallway outside the classroom.
2. Put the students in pairs. One student will be the reporter and one the writer.
3. The writer needs a pencil and paper.
4. The reporters all go to the posted paragraph, read it, and try to remember everything they can.
5. They run to their partners and report what they remember.
6. The writer writes exactly what the reporter tells.
7. The reporter runs back and forth, reading and reporting, until the paragraph is done.
8. Partners sit together to read what the writer wrote. They negotiate and discuss words, word order, spelling, and grammar.
9. Give the original, posted paragraphs to each pair to check.

Extensions: Try one of these options as a follow-up:

1. Dictate the paragraph to the students.
2. Have one partner dictate it to the other.

3. Dictate the paragraph, omitting key words for the students to fill in.

4. Students try to recreate the paragraph from memory.

5. Students write their own paragraphs, using this one as a model.

Acknowledgment: This is a variation of an activity we learned from Mario Rinvolucri during a conference.

4.5   CHAIN STORY

Because students are making up their own story, interest is high! The example given here lets students practice past verb forms. You can guide the story toward practicing other forms, or you can let the students' collective imagination take all of you for a ride.

AIM: Building confidence about writing, practicing tenses

MATERIALS: The beginning of a story

Procedure:

1. Dictate the beginning of a story to students. For example: "We went to Africa."

2. One at a time, students add a sentence in the past tense. Each student must repeat the previous sentence before adding his/her own. One story went like this: "We went to Africa. We walked to the desert. We were hot. We drank water. We were very hot. Many animals ran to the jeep. Peng killed a tiger."

3. Students write down the sentences they hear. Following are three good ways to do this, from lower proficiency level to advanced beginners. Choose the one that's best for your class:

   • As you hear each sentence, write it on the board for everyone to copy. Make the needed corrections as you go.

   • Two or more students at the board write what they hear the speaker say. The class offers suggestions for corrections if needed, then everyone copies the sentence.

   • If the sentences are simple and the students are advanced beginners, each student writes what he/she hears the speaker say, then looks at two classmates' papers to see whether they've written the same thing.

4. Each student finishes writing the story in his/her own way. Encourage them to write three to four sentences. One student wrote: "Peng killed a tiger. We made a B.B.Q. We ate the tiger."

5. In small groups, students read their stories to each other. Encourage them to read the entire story each time.

6. Each group chooses one story to be read aloud to the whole class.

7. (Optional) Post all stories for everyone to read and enjoy during the break.

Extensions:

1. Write the verbs on the board. Students may retell the story, individually or chorally. They do not look at full sentences, just at the list of verbs.

2. Use these same verbs to tell a new story in a later lesson.

4.6 THE DISAPPEARING STORY

Often, something interesting comes up in class. Perhaps Tatiana got lost yesterday, or Moto is going on a trip next week. Seize upon this as an opportunity for group writing. Interest will be high because the story is real. These stories may stick close to the truth or take off in an imaginative direction.

AIM: Composition, grammar, story-telling

MATERIALS: The beginning of a story

Procedure:

1. Start telling a story. For example, if your students have been practicing past tense, say, "Something happened to me yesterday! My doorbell rang in the middle of the night!" (Use mime if you need to.)

2. Go to the board and write the first sentence or two on one side of the board.

3. Encourage students to continue your story. As they contribute ideas, write these on the other side of the board. Use this part of the board to write what you heard the student say, including errors you want to work on. (Keep your story short; five to

six sentences will be enough.) As you go along, correct each sentence with input from the class. Then transfer each correct sentence to your "story" area of the board.

4. When the story is complete, erase the original sentences, keeping the corrected story on the board.

5. Do choral repetition of phrases.

6. Do choral repetition of full sentences.

7. In pairs, students take turns reading the story to each other.

8. While students are doing this, copy down the story. You will need this later.

9. Read the first sentence of the story. Students repeat it chorally. For example, "I jumped out of bed."

10. Erase all the words except for a key word or two. For example, "I _____ out of _____." (Make a line for each missing word.)

11. Have the class say this sentence again. (Don't say the sentence this time. Let students use the words you left on the board as prompts.)

12. Continue with other sentences in the same way.

13. Now you have a key word (or a few key words) from each sentence remaining on the board. Ask students in trios to retell the story to each other as completely as they can.

14. Each trio re-writes the story. Do this at the board, if possible; each writer will have two "coaches." Students will peek at other groups' stories as they appear on the board. This is fine because it leads to more discussion about how to reconstruct the story.

15. Go over the reconstructed stories in plenary. Point out which variations are possible ways to express the meaning and which are not possible because they change the meaning or are incorrect. This is a wonderful opportunity to point out that there's more than one correct way to express an idea!

Extension: If you wish to evaluate individual students, you may erase all the student stories, keep your version with key words on the board, and have each student rewrite the entire story to hand in to you.

Variations:

1. You can do this same activity with an announcement you want to make or a passage from your textbook.

2. You can use a picture or a series of pictures to prompt a story.

3. For a short activity, do this with a single sentence instead of a whole story.

4.7   THE VOCABULARY OF PARAGRAPHS

This activity gives students a good model of what a paragraph looks like. It also serves as a handy reference for some of the most repeated words in a beginning composition class. Because they copy the page themselves, students learn more than they would if you gave it to them as a handout. Tell them to keep it in their notebooks or folders. They can refer to it whenever they need to, for example, before handing in to you a paragraph they have written.

AIM: To learn vocabulary about the conventions of writing

Procedure:

1. Write the following paragraph on the board as students watch. (Change it to fit your situation.)

About Our Class

   We didn't come to class on Sunday because it was a holiday. Classes started on Tuesday. Jan Herron is our advisor. Jan's class is fun! I am your writing teacher, and today we will do a dictation. I think dictations are a good way to learn. Do you agree?

2. Ask, "Where is the title?" A student may come up and point it out; if not, do so yourself. Write "title" off to the side, with an arrow pointing to "About Our Class."

3. In the same way, elicit or teach the following words:

        paragraph
        first line
        indent
        capital letter
        comma
        period
        apostrophe
        question mark
        exclamation mark

When you are finished, your paragraph will look like this:

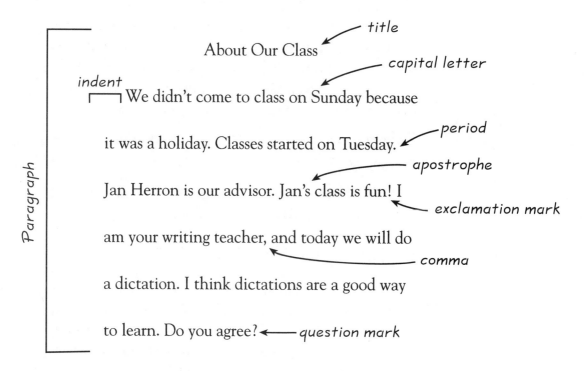

4. Point to each labeled feature of the paragraph. Say, "This is the first line." Students repeat chorally, "first line." Say, "You must indent." The class repeats, "indent." Continue through the other items in this way.

5. Go through the labeled features again. This time, say, "What is this?" as you point to each feature. The class tells you what it is.

6. Students copy the paragraph carefully, including your labels and arrows. Circulate, correcting and helping as needed.

7. Small groups review each other's work for accuracy.

8. To review, erase all your labels and arrows, leaving the original paragraph on the board. Students put their papers away and tell you what labels to put back in what places.

9. Erase the entire paragraph (or cover it). Dictate the paragraph for students to write on a fresh piece of paper. (If necessary, you may make this less challenging by leaving a few key words on the board.)

10. Students add labels to their paragraphs.

11. To check their own work, students compare their paragraphs with the labeled copy they made earlier (in step 5).

Variation: If you want students to hear these new terms again, ask such questions as "Did you indent?" "Did you remember the title?" "Did you give *Sunday* a capital 's'?" They correct their errors. (If they did it right, encourage them to raise their hands and call out, "Yes, I did!")

Extension: Do the same dictation (or a similar one) the following day. Encourage students to use their new terms as they correct their dictation in pairs.

4.8 PARTNERS IN WRITING

Writing is really speaking to a piece of paper. Students, especially beginners, often speak more naturally than they write in their target language. This may be because in writing there is more time to compose a thought in the first language, translate it mentally, then write it down (with a lot of interference errors). In this activity students speak in the target language and then immediately write. More natural language is often the result. Students also have a real audience for what they are writing. Their partner may understand (or not understand) and may be interested (or not). All of this is useful information for a writer.

One last point—this activity also gives student writers a chance to catch errors before committing words to paper.

AIM:　Producing a rough draft of a paragraph

MATERIALS:　A personal story with a universal topic

Procedure:

1. Think of a topic that your students are ready to write about. You may have read a story about families or talked about families, for example. Don't say, "We're going to write about our families." Instead, launch right into a personal story to capture their attention. For example, "I remember my grandmother. Her kitchen smelled wonderful! She gave me cookies after school." (With low beginners, use less complicated sentences.)

2. Ask questions about students' families. Get some discussion going. This can be a lot of fun! Write key words on the board.

3. Say, for example, "Raul, tell Natasha about *your* family!" Do this until everyone has a partner and all students are busily talking.

4. Bring one student up to the board to be your partner in demonstrating "Partners in Writing."

5. Say, "My grandmother was wonderful!" Write this on the board.

6. Ask your student partner, "Is this what I said? Is it correct?"

7. Speak and write two more sentences. Each time you write, ask your partner if this is what you said. For example,

    "She gave me cookies every day."

    "I love my grandmother, and I think about her a lot."

8. Now your partner does the same; he/she tells you three sentences and writes them on the board.

9. In pairs, students tell their partners' sentences about their family (or whatever subject you chose).

10. After telling each sentence, the student who spoke writes it down. Listening partners look on, helping the writer if necessary.

11. Students reread their whole paragraph to their partner.

12. Students circulate, reading their paragraph to one classmate after another.

4.9   QUESTIONS AND ANSWERS—WRITING

This activity helps students match question words with appropriate answers. It then goes further, giving students help with writing whole-sentence questions and answers correctly.

AIM: Learning what answers are appropriate to particular question words; writing whole-sentence questions and answers

MATERIALS: 3" x 5" cards or pieces of paper and tape

Procedure: (If you have done "Questions and Answers—Speaking," start with step 7.)

1. Write a few question words or phrases, each on a separate card. For example: *do, how much, who, when, where, why, how, does, what time, how many, is, are* . . .

2. Tape the cards around the room. You need to post a card on the wall for each student in your class, repeating some question words if necessary.

3. Write an answer to one of the question words on a card and hand it to a student. For example, if you are practicing *do, how much, who,* and *when,* give the following four answer cards to four different students:

| yes | $7.00 | Victor | 3:00 pm |

4. Make more answer cards (different answers to the same question words). Give these cards to other students.

5. Do this for all the students and tell them to walk around the room and look for the question word that matches their answer card.

6. When they have found their match, each student tapes his/her answer card to the bottom of the question word.

7. Everyone sits down.

8. Take the cards off the wall, keeping the question/answer pairs taped together.

9. Hand a pair of cards to each student.

10. Using these prompts, each student writes (on his/her own paper) a question and an answer in complete sentences.

11. When students are finished, they hold up their cards to trade with someone who is also finished.

12. Students keep exchanging and writing until time is up.

13. Collect the papers. When you read them, you will see what your students need to practice more.

See "Let's Correct Those Mistakes," Chapter 4, page 50, for a whole-class sentence correction activity.

4.10 REVISION: I CAN DO IT MYSELF!

This can be done after "The Vocabulary of Paragraphs," Chapter 4, page 55.

This routine saves the composition teacher a great deal of time by strengthening students' internal correctness "monitors." They learn to correct "old" errors before handing in a new piece of writing. The teacher is thus free to concentrate on helping students with new errors as they improve their writing.

AIM: Improving students' ability to edit their own work

MATERIALS: A stapler, a simple two-pocket folder for each student (This will hold formal compositions but no other work.)

Procedure:

1. Students write their names on the outside of their folders.

2. Write on the board in big, block letters these two sentences:

    "I do these things correctly."

    "I checked these things and I am ready to give my composition to my teacher."

3. Each student writes the first sentence at the top of a clean piece of paper and the second sentence at the bottom:

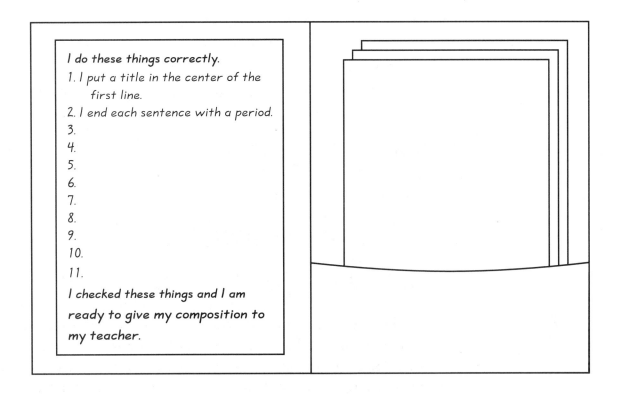

4. Pass around a stapler. Students staple their papers on the left inside of their folders.

5. Ask students what they can do correctly in their compositions. To help them get started, write on the board such ideas as:

    "I put a title in the center of the first line."

    "I begin each sentence with a capital letter."

    "I end each sentence with a period."

    "I indent the first line of a paragraph."

6. Students write the number "1" on their paper and copy from the list on the board something they know they can *always* do correctly. (They should add an example of each.) They continue listing more things, with each student including only what he/she is sure they will never do incorrectly in a paper they hand in.

7. This paper remains in the folder throughout your course, along with successive drafts of assigned compositions. Each time a student masters something, offer congratulations and

ask whether she or he wants to add it to their list. It is important that students, not you, choose what goes on their lists.

8. Before students hand in each composition, give them class time to use their lists in editing their work. Encourage them to look for only one error at a time. This will take some modeling and persistence until students notice for themselves how many errors they miss when they read their work globally. (Classmates can help!)

9. While this is going on, circulate. Point to the list, not the composition, if you see an error. The student has claimed mastery of this and should be able to find that error in his/her own composition.

10. When students finally hand in their folders, they are, in effect, assuring you that they have taken responsibility for the errors on their personal lists. Sometimes it is possible to scan compositions as they are handed in. If a student has missed an error listed on his or her list, don't accept the composition.

11. As you are correcting their work, you have each student's list in front of you, stapled into his/her folder. It takes very little time to scan it before reading the composition. If you do find an error that a student has claimed mastery of but did not correct, you have options:

    •   You can simply stop reading and return that paper to the student.

    •   You may (or may not) automatically adjust the grade.

4.11   IMAGINARY GIFT EXCHANGE

This activity touches the place in the heart that loves to give (and receive!) the perfect gift. Use this after students know each other well; it makes a fine last-day activity!

AIM: Letter-writing, vocabulary building, practicing *why* and *because*

MATERIALS: Something to put slips of paper in (a small box, basket, bag, or hat)

Procedure:

1. Together with the class, create a list on the board of things that people like to give and receive as presents. Include real and fantasy gifts, for example:

a red sports car
more time
help with homework
a handsome (or rich) husband
a rich (or beautiful) wife
a trip to Japan to visit me
your lost keys

2. On the board write the following formula:

```
September 23 (put actual date here)


Dear _____,


I am giving you _____ for a
present because _____.


Yours,


_____
```

3. Choose a gift that students will understand the reason for. For example, if Saleh has been using a tiny stub of a pencil for two weeks, hold up a new pencil for all to see. Say, "Why am I giving Saleh a new pencil? I am giving Saleh a new pencil because he has an old pencil."

4. Turn to the formula you wrote on the board, fill it in, and sign your name.

5. Practice this formula a few times orally, using various student names, gifts, and reasons. (Continue to use *why* and *because*.)

6. To make sure that everyone gets a present, every student puts his or her name on a slip of paper and drops it into the box. Students choose a name at random. (If they pick their own name, they take a different slip.)

7. Each student writes a gift note to the person whose name he/she chose. Circulate, offering help as needed. (Encourage creativity; this is your opportunity to do vocabulary expansion as well.)

8. Students deliver their gift notes.

9. Students return the name slip to the box.

10. After everyone has read their notes, introduce thank-you notes. Use the formula below and follow steps 2 through 5.

September 23 (put actual date here)

Dear _____,

Thank you very much for _____
_____. I like it because
_____.

Yours,

_____

---

11. Students write their thank-you notes and deliver them to the gift-giver.

12. Continue the activity, with students writing to classmate after classmate, stopping to write thank-you notes each time they receive a gift.

13. When it's time to stop, students display all of their gift notes and thank-you notes on their desks. (If any note is private, of course, they put it away.)

14. Students walk around reading other people's notes. This is great fun! It's also a way to talk about the vocabulary they find in other people's notes.

Extension: Write the new words on the board. Or copy them into your notebook and re-use them in another activity later.

4.12 LEARN THOSE LETTERS!

Here's an activity that helps students who are learning a new alphabet.

This activity can be followed by "Wall Dictionary," Chapter 5, page 69.

AIM: Teaching letters

Procedure:

1. Teach the letters a few at a time. Write each one on the board as you say its name and make the sound of that letter.
2. Students repeat each letter chorally and individually.
3. Students "write" each letter in the air as they name and make the sound of the letter.
4. Students stand in a long line and trace each letter on the back of a classmate as you say the name and make the sound of that letter.
5. After introducing a few letters, start pointing to old ones on the board, inviting students to recall them and repeating steps 2 through 4. Try for a 90% success rate; if students succeed in recalling the letters you've already practiced, introduce another one.

Chapter Five
Vocabulary

Learning new words is the first aim of a beginning language learner. Words are the building blocks that help us build our new language "house." Words in a new language feel strange and awkward on our tongues. We need to "meet" them many times before they sound normal and friendly, and we need to say them many times before they can serve our purposes. We need repetition and a lot of it, but repetition can become very boring. That is why this book has many varied techniques that will help our students to master their new words.

5.1   ALL THE WORDS WE KNOW

This activity works well on the first day of class when many students feel intimidated by the new language and are sure that everyone knows more than they do. Individual students are surprised by how many words they already know. The activity also builds group cohesion, giving students a sense of belonging.

 **AIM:**   Building confidence

Procedure:

1. Say, "We are going to learn many new words, but you already know many words. You know words like *telephone, television,* and *okay.*" Add a few other appropriate words that your students may know.

2. In small groups, students write down all the words that they already know or think they know.

3. A volunteer from one of the groups reads out one word. If students in the other groups have the same word, they cross it off their lists. Put this word on the board.

4. The next group repeats step 3.

5. Continue until all words are on the board.

6. Review all these words and praise the students for their knowledge.

Variation: For low beginners (students who cannot easily write the words they know), stand at the board and ask the whole class to call out words they know. Write these on the board.

5.2 WALL DICTIONARY

Here's another good activity for students who are learning a new alphabet. You also gain a permanent display of the alphabet in your room, with a growing collection of words the students are learning. You'll refer to this chart again and again.

MATERIALS: Pieces of paper, tape

AIM: Formation (handwriting) and letter recognition

Procedure:

1. Post the letters around the room (or write them on the board), both in capital and small forms (see illustration).

2. When attendance is called, students write their names on pieces of paper and post them under the correct letter.

3. Each time you introduce a new word, a student writes it on a piece of paper and posts it under the correct letter.

4. Periodically, ask students to read the words written under the letters. Doing this gives students a good review of the sound each letter represents.

5. Periodically remove all papers under the letters and scramble them.

6. Students sort papers and replace them in the right columns. (This is where handwriting becomes important. If students can't read what another student wrote, everyone will learn something about how to form that letter correctly.)

Aa	Bb	Cc	Dd	Ee
Alfredo	Blanca	Carmen	Daud	Ernesto
apple	boy	cookie	dog	elephant
are	bread	cat	daddy	egg

5.3 DISAPPEARING VOCABULARY

This game is challenging and fun! It gives students plenty of practice saying new words and seeing how they are spelled, while the playful urgency of trying to remember the disappearing words keeps everyone's energy high.

 **AIM:** Reviewing vocabulary

Procedure:

1. After students have learned the meanings of some new words, list them on the board.

2. Point to each word and say it. Students repeat each word chorally.

3. Repeat the whole list in order several times, pointing to the words and saying them for the class to repeat.

4. Continue pointing at words, but on some words do not speak. Let students say the word without modeling it for them. Go through the list again and again, saying fewer words each time, until students are reading the entire list, as you point at each word, with no help from you.

5. Go faster each time through the list.

6. Point to a word, let the class say it, then erase it and have them say it again. (You have just made this word disappear.) The first time you do this, students will be surprised!

7. Continue going through the list several more times, erasing another word from time to time. Point to each empty place so the class says the entire list, both visible words and invisible words. Keep the pace quick.

8. By the end of the activity, all words have been erased. Students have memorized the list and are calling it out as you point to the blank spaces on the board.

9. Invite three students to come to the board and rewrite the list as classmates call out the words. If someone spells a word wrong, classmates call out the correct spelling.

5.4   **FROM PICTURES TO WORDS**

This activity is a powerful way to learn new words. Students choose for themselves pictures of things they want to know the names of. Then they practice their new words using eyes, ears, and physical activity. Plus you get a set of flashcards!

AIM: Vocabulary development

MATERIALS: Magazines and catalogs with pictures in them (brought by you or your students), tape to attach pictures to paper from the students' notebooks, scissors (optional because students can tear out pictures)

Procedure:

1. Students cut out (or tear out) pictures of objects that interest them. With dictionaries, classmates, and you as resources, they write their name and the name of each object on a piece of paper and clip this to each picture. Walk around, helping with pronunciation.

2. Each student stands up with one of their pictures.
3. The student finds a partner, looks at his/her picture, and asks, "What is this?"
4. The partner replies, for example, "It's a hammer."
5. After teaching and learning, they exchange papers and go find a new partner.
6. Continue until most students know most of the words.
7. Gather all the pictures. Use them as flash cards; show each picture as students name the object chorally and individually.

5.5 TWO UNRELATED PICTURES

It is always a mental adventure to find similarities in things that looked very different at first glance. Even beginners can experience this "Aha!" when you use pictures to generate vocabulary.

AIM: Vocabulary development

MATERIALS: Several pictures of objects (if you've done the activity, "From Pictures to Words," Chapter 5, page 71, use the pictures the students chose.)

Procedure:

1. Choose two unrelated pictures, for example, a hammer and a chair. Hold them up and ask the class, "How are these the same?"

2. Volunteers answer, saying, for example, "They are brown. They are new. They are in a house. You use them."

3. Help students formulate sentences and write them on the board, like this:

      hammer, chair   They are brown.

4. A student chooses two other unrelated pictures and holds them up for the class to find something in common.

5. Do a few more rounds, with other students choosing pairs of unrelated pictures.

6. As you go along, continue writing the items and what they have in common on the board, like this:

      hammer, chair   They are brown.
      dog, tree   They are outside the house.
      computer disk, house   They are square.

7. In small groups, students use the words on the right side of the board. For example, they list as many things as they can possibly think of that are brown. They make another list of things outside the house, etc. When they are done, the students are amazed at how many words they know in their target language.

Variation: Choose two similar pictures. For example, choose two pictures of chairs and ask, "How are these different?" This will generate words like *small* and *large*, *old* and *new*, etc.

5.6 SPELLING IMPROVEMENT

In this activity, students spell vocabulary words by moving around letters that have been written on small pieces of paper. Students fix their own spelling if they get it wrong at first, thus learning, in the process, which words they need to study more.

AIM: Improve spelling of any previously taught vocabulary.

MATERIALS: Small squares of paper (about 2" x 2"), a list of the spelling words you want your students to practice. For example:

ear	back
face	neck
nose	foot
arm	feet
stomach	

Procedure:

1. Identify which letters students will need to spell the list of words by following the steps below. (This will take you about three minutes. You may do it before class or while students are working on their own.)

    -   Quickly go down the list, starting at the word below *ear*.

    -   Cross out the e's, a's and r's in the rest of the words. If there are two of the same letters in a word, as in *feet*, just cross out one of them. (Students will need both "e's" to spell *feet*.)

    -   Below the second word, *face*, cross out the f's and c's in words three through nine.

    -   Continue until your list looks like this:

ear	ba̸c̸k
fa̸c̸e̸	n̸e̸c̸k
nose̸	f̸o̸ot̸
a̸r̸m	f̸e̸et̸
st̸o̸m̸a̸c̸h	

Now you know the letters that the students will need to spell the vocabulary words. In this case they are: *e, a, r, f, c, n, o, s, m, t, h, b, k, o, e.*

2. Write these letters on the board.

3. Each student copies all the letters, putting each letter onto a small square of paper. (They may cut or tear paper squares.)

4. Dictate each vocabulary word. The students move their letters around on their desks to spell each word.

5. For each word, walk around the room and check each student. Give them a "thumbs up" for correct spelling, "thumbs down" if they need to try again.

6. Ask questions to make sure the students understand the meaning. For example, "Where is your ear?"

Extension: Ask, "How do you spell *ear?*" Call on a student who first got it wrong and then corrected it. He/she dictates the spelling and you write the word on the board. Continue with other words and other students.

Variation: Make only one set of letters and pass them out to the students until all the letters are gone. Dictate a word. The students with letters for that word must run to the front of the room, face the other students and get in the correct order to spell the word. Let the audience decide if the word is correct.

Note: Keep the "letter sets" you have made for particular groups of words (parts of the body, for example). You can use them for later review or with another group of students.

5.7 PICTURES ON OUR BACKS

Everyone keeps moving and speaking in this boisterous vocabulary builder!

AIM: Speaking, listening, descriptions

MATERIALS: Pictures in a certain category (for example: food or animals), tape

Procedure:

1. Hold up a picture so the students can see it and say, "I will tell you about this picture." Don't say the name of the object in the picture, just describe it. If you are using food, talk about tastes (*sour, sweet, salty, bland*). Ways to eat it are also good (*cooked, raw, in a salad*). If you are using animals, you could say where it lives, whether it is wild or a pet, what color it is, if it has a long tail, big ears, etc.

2. Write new vocabulary on the board as you are describing the picture.

3. Describe another picture to the class, this time not showing the picture.

4. Write new vocabulary on the board as you are describing the second picture.

5. Students guess what the object in the second picture is.

6. Repeat with several more pictures until there is a good selection of words on the board.

7. Divide the class in two groups, the "apples" and the "bananas."

8. The apples stand, facing the board with the vocabulary on it.

9. Spread out all your pictures on a table or on desks.

10. Each banana chooses a picture, goes to stand behind an apple, and tapes the picture to the back of the apple partner. (If there's an extra student, he/she can join a pair and be either an extra apple or an extra banana.)

11. The banana describes the picture, and the apple guesses what the object is until the answer is correct.

12. The banana takes the picture off the partner's back, shows it to him/her, and replaces it in the pile of pictures.

13. Partners trade roles and repeat steps 8 through 12.

14. The game goes on until the class is tired.

5.8 WALLET TALK

Students share a little of themselves with their classmates in this highly entertaining activity. Even low beginners can produce some good vocabulary with the help of the rest of the group. You can use this short activity as a time-filler at the beginning or end of a class, or you can use it as a prelude to another activity.

 **AIM:** Building vocabulary, speaking, listening

Procedure:

1. Talk with the class about wallets, purses, backpacks, book bags—anything that we use to carry items around.

2. Ask students to find something interesting or unique in their wallet, purse, or pack. They could have a picture, money, a key, a religious item or a good luck charm. A pen could even be interesting if it has a story. Give them a few minutes to make a choice.

3. If the class is large, divide students into groups of three or four. If it is small, you can do this all together.

4. Ask each student to tell everything he/she knows about the chosen object. Pass it around and let others see it and ask questions. The class or group can work together to get the maximum vocabulary out of an object.

Extension: For class cohesion, recycle the new vocabulary by asking questions regarding what students said about their possessions. For example:

> "Whose picture is this?"
> "Who is in the picture?"
> "Why does he carry it in his wallet?"

Note: After you have done this once, you can ask students to bring in something they'd like to speak about. They do not have to prepare a speech, just bring something that might interest others.

5.9 **DESCRIPTIONS I**

This is an excellent activity for building vocabulary to later use in extended activities.

AIM: Vocabulary building, speaking, listening

MATERIALS: Pictures in a category (Any category will do, such as animals, clothing, vacation places, etc.)

Procedure:

1. Hold up one picture and ask, "Who can tell me about this picture?"

2. Write words on the board as the students say them, in no particular order.

3. Repeat steps one and two several times with new pictures.

4. After there are quite a few words on the board, students look at all of them and see if there are any that belong under the same heading. (For example, if your main category is "faces," group words together under headings like hair, colors, cheeks, eyes, nose, etc.)

5. Write these headings on the board. Student volunteers come to the board and, with the help of the whole class, write the words under the correct heading.

6. When the words have been placed under the right heading, all students copy them into their notebooks to keep.

7. In pairs, students drill one another on vocabulary by covering up the words under a heading, leaving only the heading, and letting their partners orally recreate the list.

hair	eyes	cheeks	nose	other words
blonde	blue	rosy	long	beard
black	green	pink	short	moustache
brown	brown	big		
red	hazel	small		
gray				
salt and pepper				
curly				
straight				

5.10   DESCRIPTIONS II: HAVE YOU SEEN MY GRANDMOTHER?

With all the action going on in this activity, students get better and faster at describing pictures.

You may want to do "Descriptions I," Chapter 5, page 77, before this activity.

AIM: Asking and answering questions, using descriptive adjectives, listening, reinforcing new vocabulary, using *be* and *have*

MATERIALS: Various pictures in a category that contains words students already know

Procedure:

1. Spread out all the pictures.

2. Write the following frames on the board so the students can refer to them:

   Have you seen my _____?

   She/he/it has _____.

   Is this your _____? She/he/it has _____.

   No, my _____ has _____.

   Yes, that is my _____.

3. Separate the class into two groups, for example, lions and tigers. Students pair up; each pair has one lion and one tiger.

4. Once they know who their partner is, send all the tigers to one side of the room and all the lions to the other side.

5. Lions walk to the table, study all the pictures, and mentally choose one.

6. Lions go back to their tiger partners and tell them one sentence about the picture they have chosen, for example "Have you seen my grandmother? She has gray hair."

7. The tiger goes to the pictures and chooses the one he/she thinks is correct. The tiger takes it to the lion partner and asks if it is the correct picture, repeating the lion's describing sentence. For example: "Is this your grandmother? She has gray hair."

8. If it is not the correct picture, the lion adds more information. For example: "No, my grandmother has short, gray hair."

9. If it is the correct picture, the lion acknowledges it. For example: "Yes, that is my grandmother."

10. Partners change places and do the activity again and again, for as long as interest is high.

Variation: If the students are low beginners, the teacher can be the lion and all the students can be tigers.

5.11   STICKS AND STONES—PRACTICING NUMBERS

Students love this noisy, fun game from South America because it touches their gambling spirit. After the students understand the simple rules, they can run the game by themselves, leaving the teacher free to roam and listen for correct numbers and pronunciation.

AIM: Practicing numbers, pronouncing numbers, review

MATERIALS: Any small objects that can be held in one hand, for example: paper clips, small pieces of paper (we use toothpicks broken in pieces); small prizes (we use small stones)

Procedure:

1. Give an equal number of "sticks" (for example, three) to each student.

2. Put the pile of small "stones" where everyone can see them.

3. Each student takes their three sticks, hides them under their desk, and puts zero, one, two, or three sticks in one hand.

4. All students put the hand with the sticks hidden inside on the top of their desk. They must not show their sticks!

5. Each person guesses the total number of sticks in all the hands. In a class of ten, the highest possible number is thirty. Students must pronounce numbers clearly, so all can understand the correct guess. (Don't write the number on the board. Let them misunderstand each other and work to pronounce numbers more clearly.)

6. After all guesses are in, a volunteer counts the sticks (a good learning activity in itself!) The volunteer awards a "stone" as a prize to the student with the closest guess.

7. Students change the number of sticks they're holding for each round of the game.

8. To stop the game, everyone counts their stones to see who is the winner. (This is a chance to introduce the words *lucky* and *unlucky*.)

Note: Vary the number of sticks occasionally to change the totals. (You may, for example, give everyone four sticks instead of three.)

Variation: For large classes play in small groups. Once students understand it, this game runs itself.

5.12 WHAT AM I DRAWING?

This fast-paced drawing activity is a real "class-pleaser!" It has the flexibility to be a team or individual game, with points or without. It allows students with limited vocabulary to use their knowledge and creativity. It is a twist on the popular game, "Pictionary."

AIM: Recycling and expanding previously taught vocabulary, fast thinking, speaking

MATERIALS: A vocabulary list based on a certain theme or aspect of language (for example: action verbs, irregular verbs, emotions, words about food)

Procedure:

1. Tell the students what vocabulary list you have chosen. They should not have the lists in front of them.
2. One student joins you outside of the class where the others can't hear.
3. Tell that student one word from your list.
4. Tell him/her to draw a picture of that word on the board. *Key point: They must not speak or gesture!*
5. The student must draw until someone guesses the correct word.
6. That person gets one point.
7. The winning person gets other points if he/she can expand the word in some way. This expansion will vary according to the words you have chosen to use. For instance, if you are using irregular past tense verbs, like *draw*, the winner gets one point for *draw*, one point for knowing the past tense, *drew*, and another point for using it correctly in a sentence. If you are

using adjectives, the winner may get a point for the word, *old*, another point for using it correctly in a sentence, and another one for knowing its opposite, *young*.

8. If the winner can't expand, he/she only gets one point and volunteers from the class expand.

9. Choose a new student and start over with a new word.

Note: If your students are low beginners, use nouns because they're easier to draw and guess. Less concrete words, like adjectives or irregular past tense verbs, are more fun, but also more challenging.

5.13 BIRTHDAY LINEUP

Students lose those "first-few-days jitters," get acquainted, and gather information about each other in this physical activity.

 **AIM:** Ordinal numbers, months and their correct order in the year, students' names

Procedure:

1. Say the months of the year.
2. The class repeats chorally.
3. Say some ordinal numbers, for example: *first, second, third . . .*
4. The class repeats chorally.
5. Write all the months and some ordinal numbers on the board.
6. The class reads the months and numbers chorally.
7. Choose a student and ask, "What is your name?"
8. The student responds, "My name is _____." (for example, Isslemou)
9. Ask, "Isslemou, when is your birthday?"
10. Help him make his answer into the sentence, "My birthday is February 10th."
11. This student stands and comes to the front of the classroom, facing the other students.
12. Ask the other students, "What is his name?"
13. The students respond, "His name is Isslemou."
14. Write his name on the board, if there is confusion.

15. Ask the students, "When is Isslemou's birthday?"

16. They answer, "February 10th" or "His birthday is February 10th." or "It is February 10th." You decide how you want them to answer.

17. Choose another student and repeat steps 7-16.

18. Ask the class, "Does _____ (the birthday of the second student) come before or after February 10th?"

19. The class answers chorally.

20. If it comes before, the student stands in front of Isslemou. If after, the student stands behind him.

21. Repeat with all the students (or up to fifteen, if your class is large) until there is one long line with the birthday months and days in the correct order.

22. Ask for volunteers to say everyone's name and birthday.

Note: If someone has a birthday during the class session, plan a party!

5.14 A, B, C VOCABULARY GAME

Lift the spirits of your beginning students by showing them how many words they know! With this activity, students leave the class feeling great!

AIM: Vocabulary building and review, cooperation

MATERIALS: A picture with many objects in it for each group of two or three students, or a collection of varied pictures for each group

Procedure:

1. In groups of two or three, students write the alphabet, listing the letters A through Z on a piece of paper, going down the left side, and skipping two lines between letters.

2. Give each group a picture (or a group of pictures).

3. Students work together to list as many words as they can, using the pictures, under the correct beginning letter. For example, under A they may write *airplane, apple tree, arm, artist*, etc.

4. Set a time to finish or let them work until they can think of no more words.

5. Each group leaves its list and pictures and moves to another group's list and pictures.

6. Each group looks at the new list and pictures and tries to match the words and the pictures. That is, they see *apple* on the list and find the apple in the picture.

7. They can also add new words to the list.

8. Move the groups several times if interest is still high.

9. Groups go back to their original list. They see what words were added, find these things in their picture(s), and count the total number of words.

10. Write the totals on the board, and add them to get a grand total.

11. Celebrate because the class knows so many words!

5.15 YOU ARE VERY BEAUTIFUL!

Everyone in the class gets a self-esteem boost from this activity!

 **AIM:**   Giving compliments with adjectives and intensifiers

Procedure:

1. When the class begins, select a student and say, "You are _____." (Choose an adjective, for example: *beautiful, handsome, smart, wonderful*.)

2. Turn to another student and ask, "Do you think he/she is _____?"

3. Tell them in a whisper to answer, "Yes."

4. Write the compliment on the board, for example: "Lorenza is beautiful."

5. Tell the students that this is a true statement, but not true enough.

6. Add *very* before the adjective.

7. Ask, "What is a different way to make this strong?"

8. Write "Lorenza is extremely beautiful!"

9. Write "Lorenza is really beautiful!"

10. Bring up a male student and repeat steps 1 through 9, using *handsome*.

11. Talk about adjectives and intensifiers. (Say, "Adjectives describe people. Intensifiers make the adjective stronger.")

12. Write adjectives and intensifiers on the board in two separate columns.

Adjectives	Intensifiers
beautiful	very
handsome	extremely
young	really
interesting	
funny	
nice	
good	

13. Add more adjectives and use different students' names, saying and writing on the board sentences such as:

"Murat, you are extremely intelligent."

"Masa, you are very young and really healthy."

14. Talk about the meanings of the adjectives.

15. Students look them up in their dictionaries, if necessary.

16. Students practice giving each other compliments.

17. Each student writes his/her name on a slip of paper.

18. Collect these; then hand out one name to each student (not their own name).

19. Each student writes a compliment to the classmate whose name they were given, then signs it. Write this model on the board:

Dear _____,

You are _____ _____.

Your friend,

_____

20. Students deliver their notes. The happy recipients tuck these away in their billfold or purse.

Acknowledgement: This is a variation of an activity we learned from Joel Laing. Thank you, Joel!

5.16 VOCABULARY CARDS

Ask students what they need, and most will give you the same answer: more words!

They are right! Here is an activity that helps them remember and reuse the words they are learning, recycling them to form new associations as your course goes along. This works better for many students than writing lists in a notebook because:

- They can post cards on their refrigerator, their bathroom mirror, etc.
- They can throw away cards once they've mastered a word.
- They can use the cards as flashcards for review (they see the word but can't see the definition until they turn the card over).

AIM: Reviewing vocabulary

MATERIALS: Enough index cards to give each student three or four (Later they can buy their own cards.)

Procedure:

1. Every time students want to remember a word they just learned, they make a vocabulary card. (3" x 5" index cards work well.) On the front, the student prints the new word, as large as possible. On the back the student puts anything that will help him/her remember the meaning (pictures, translations, similar words or opposites, notes about pronunciation or part of speech, etc.). Every card must also have a short sentence in the target language using the new word correctly.

2. Students use these as flashcards, quizzing themselves independently (in class and at home) by looking at the front and trying to remember the word, then using it in a sentence. If they need help, they can look on the back.

Variations:

1. In class, pairs play a card game in which they fan out their own collection of flashcards for their partner to see. The partner points to a card at random, and the holder uses the word in a sentence. This game can be given a competitive edge if small coins are won or lost when a student succeeds or fails to remember a word.

2. Students take out all their cards and arrange them into categories, then explain to a classmate why they sorted them in this way. (Typical categories might be colors, furniture, parts of the body, clothing, etc.)

5.17 MAKE THE WORD GO AWAY

This routine really makes words stick in students' memories. Use this with foods, colors, numbers, parts of the body, or any kind of vocabulary you want to practice.

AIM: Review, vocabulary study

MATERIALS: Recently taught vocabulary words, each written on a large piece of paper. Make one word-paper for each student. (It's okay to use a word more than once.)

Procedure:

1. Give each student a word-paper.
2. In pairs, each student holds up his/her paper and the other shows or tells the meaning.
3. Students switch partners and repeat step two a few times.
4. Circulate around the class, choosing words you feel need to be reviewed. Pick up these word-papers.
5. Post these words in a place where the whole class can see them.
6. Class reviews these words by reading them out and telling or showing their meanings. (This can be done both chorally and individually.)
7. Students close their eyes.
8. Remove one of the words and rearrange the others.

9. Students open their eyes and put up a hand as soon as they know which word has been removed.

10. Call on a student to say the missing word, and the class repeats it chorally.

Variation: You can turn this activity into a competitive game. After steps 1 through 4, try this:

1. Appoint a score keeper.

2. Divide the class into two teams.

3. Each team sends a representative to the front of the room.

4. The two representatives turn their backs to the posted words.

5. A member of the class removes one word and rearranges the rest.

6. The team representatives turn to the words.

7. The first representative to spot and shout out the missing word scores a point for his/her team.

Note: This game can get very noisy.

5.18 CAN YOU SMELL IT?

This routine energizes students and brings a lot of laughs. Use it to review foods, colors, numbers, parts of the body, or any other words.

AIM: Vocabulary review, question formation, teaching *taste, smell, feel,* and *listen*

MATERIALS: A scarf or piece of material to blindfold student; recently taught vocabulary words, each written on a large piece of paper

Procedure:

1. Give each student a word-paper.

2. In pairs, each student holds up his/her paper and the other shows or tells the meaning.

3. Students switch partners and repeat step 2 a few times.

4. Circulate around the class, choosing words you feel need to be reviewed. Pick up these word-papers.

5. Bring a lively student to the front of the room and blindfold him/her.

6. A volunteer brings up his/her word-paper, shows it to the whole class, and hands it to the blindfolded student.

7. The blindfolded student smells, feels, tastes, listens to the paper crinkle. (This is just good fun!)

8. The blindfolded student asks questions to get at the meaning of the word. Examples:

> "Is it an action?"
> "Is it good to eat?"
> "Is it yellow?"

9. The class shouts out answers.

10. If after ten guesses, the blindfolded student still has not guessed the word, the class gives hints until the student guesses or gives up.

Extension: With an extra blindfold, you can turn this activity into a competitive game. After steps 1-4, try this:

5. Appoint a score keeper.

6. Divide class into two teams.

7. Each team sends a representative to the front of the room.

8. Blindfold both representatives.

9. Choose a word-paper.

10. One representative asks three questions about the word, then the other asks three questions.

11. Turn taking continues until one guesses correctly and scores a point for his/her team.

Note: This game can get very noisy.

5.19 THE HOKEY POKEY

This is a highly enjoyable activity that pumps up energy and is enjoyed by both children and adults. Here are the words for "The Hokey Pokey:"

> You put your right foot in,
> You take your right foot out
> You put your right foot in,
> And you shake it all about.
> You do "The Hokey Pokey"
> And you turn yourself around.
> That's what it's all about!

AIM: Reviewing parts of the body and *right* and *left*

Procedure:

1. Class stands in a circle.

2. Demonstrate the song, putting your foot into the circle, picking it up, and shaking it about as you sing.

3. Turn around, waving your hands above your head as you sing "You do *The Hokey Pokey* and you turn yourself around."

4. Face the students and clap your hands as you sing, "That's what it's all about!"

5. Students join you in the actions, singing along with as many words as they can. (Go over each line more than once.)

6. Use other parts of the body (your hand, your elbow, etc.). This is a time to ham it up and be silly. After reviewing the main parts of the body, try things like:

   > "Put an eye in"
   > "Put your tummy in"
   > "Put your fanny in"

7. Invite a student to lead the singing and action. The student decides what part of the body to do.

8. This student invites another student, who invites yet another classmate to lead the song and action.

9. Continue until parts of the body have been used many times.

10. To conclude the game, use this line: "Put your whole self in, take your whole self out." The motion here is a jump into and out of the circle.

Note: If you don't want to sing this, just do it as a chant.

5.20 SALAD BOWL

This variation of musical chairs allows students to review vocabulary while they move around and laugh a bit.

 **AIM:**   Class cohesion, energy raising, vocabulary review

Procedure:

1. Students sit in a circle.
2. Assign a vegetable name to each student. No more than five names should be used. Example: *radish, cucumber, lettuce, tomato, onion.*
3. Explain the meaning of these vegetables by drawing or asking talented students to draw. You can also show pictures.
4. Shout the name of a vegetable, such as "Tomato!"
5. All the students who have been assigned this name jump up and exchange seats.
6. As students jump up, remove one of the chairs in the circle.
7. The student who is left without a chair is the one who calls out the next vegetable name.
8. The game continues until only one student is left.
9. When you shout, "Salad bowl!" all students must jump and exchange seats.
10. Quickly review the meanings.

Extension: Choose a new set of vegetables and play the game again.

Variation: This game can be used to review any vocabulary category. If you're reviewing animal names, call it "The Zoo." If furniture, "The Furniture Store." If relationships, "The Family."

5.21 WHO IS THIS?

Describing how someone looks is not easy. Students enjoy themselves in this activity while learning a lot of necessary vocabulary.

Steps 14 and 15 could touch sensitive territory, so you may want to do the activity, "You are Very Beautiful!," Chapter 5, page 83, first to get descriptions going on a positive note.

AIM: Reviewing facial features

MATERIALS: A copy of the ten faces for each student

Procedure:

1. Each student chooses one of the faces to describe. He/she doesn't tell anyone which face they have chosen.

2. Students look carefully at their chosen face and write as many words as they can that describe the picture.

3. Each student describes the picture, speaking quietly to him/herself while looking at it.

4. Students practice in the same way again, this time without looking at the picture.

5. One student volunteers to describe the face he/she has chosen. He/she describes the face as completely as possible. (No one is to interrupt until this description is complete.)

6. Students who think they know which picture was described raise their hands and guess. (They look at the pictures while listening.)

7. The student who described the picture says which guess is correct.

8. Ask if any other student also picked this picture.

9. Those who did raise their hands.

10. Ask if the student who described the picture forgot anything.

11. The other students who picked the same picture add information.

12. A new volunteer describes a new face. Repeat the procedure several times.

13. In pairs, students practice choosing faces, describing them and identifying them.

14. One student at a time volunteers to describe a member of the class, while the class guesses who this could be.

15. Students continue this activity in pairs.

Extension: If you wish, have students write a composition describing someone in the class. The compositions are posted on the walls of the class for everyone to admire.

Variation: You can use this routine with houses, furnished rooms, or store shelves if you have pictures.

5.22 ARITHMETIC FUN

This activity gives those students who have always loved arithmetic a sense of pleasure and power in their new language.

AIM: Reviewing numbers

Procedure:

1. Put any two-digit number on the board, for example: 14.
2. Put on the board _____ + _____ = 14
3. Get students to help you do the arithmetic.
4. Put on the board _____ + _____ = 14 and elicit a new combination to equal 14.
5. In small groups, students write down any combinations they can think of whose total is 14. Examples: 10 + 4, 7 + 7, 6 + 8.
6. Stop when you notice that many students have finished their combinations.
7. Call on any student to read out any *one* number combination on his/her list.
8. Students who have this number combination cross it out.
9. Continue until all number combinations have been read.
10. The student left with a combination that no one else wrote is declared the winner.

Note: Be ready to use more complex numbers and other operations as soon as your students are ready for more of a challenge.

5.23 WHAT DAY IS IT TODAY?

This activity creates a classroom ritual and establishes a friendly and supportive classroom community. You may want to do this (or parts of it) every day!

AIM: Reviewing days of the week, months of the year, and seasons of the year; reviewing numbers; establishing classroom ritual

MATERIALS: Large calendar

Procedure:

1. Place a large calendar in the front of the class.
2. Call on one student to read the days of the week.
3. Ask, "What day is it today?" Volunteers answer.
4. Ask, "What day was it yesterday?" Volunteers answer.
5. Ask, "What day will it be tomorrow?" Volunteers answer.
6. Ask, "What month is it now? What number is this month in the year?" Elicit several correct responses. Insist on cardinal numbers, for example: "the third month, the sixth month."
7. Ask, "What season is this?" Elicit responses.
8. Ask, "When is your birthday? What day? What month? What season?"
9. Ask, "What is your favorite season?"
10. Eliciting help from students, write all the above questions on the board.
11. In pairs, students ask each other the questions and answer them.

5.24 OUR BIRTHDAYS

This activity works on many levels and helps to create a supportive classroom community.

 AIM: Review of dates (with ordinal numbers) and names of months

Procedure:

1. Elicit the names of the months and write them on the board.
2. Ask, "Saung Hwa, when is your birthday?"
3. Write his response on the board, for example: "June twenty-second (or 22nd)."
4. Repeat steps 2 and 3 with several students.
5. Students stand and mingle, asking each other, "When is your birthday?"
6. When students sit again ask, "Who remembers when Sandra's birthday is?"
7. Get a response.

8. Repeat with several students.

9. Ask, "Who has a birthday in January?"

10. Repeat with several other months.

11. Teach the "Happy Birthday" song and sing it for those students who have birthdays in the present month.

5.25 WORKING WITH MONEY

This game-like activity teaches the names of monetary units and brings about a lot of laughs.

AIM: Teaching the names of coins, practicing numbers

MATERIALS: A quarter, a dime, a nickel, a penny, a dollar bill, a five-dollar bill, a ten-dollar bill, and a twenty-dollar bill

Procedure:

1. Hold up each piece of money, say its name, and write it on the board.

2. The whole class repeats each one several times.

3. Call on single students to say these words.

4. Give one piece of money to each of several students.

5. Say, "Pedro, please come and put the dime on the table."

6. Continue until all the money is back on the table.

7. Ask new students to pick up money. "Maria, please come and get the dime," etc.

8. Ask a student to pass their money to another student, for example: "Petra, please give your dollar to Anima."

9. Continue until the students know the names of these monetary units reasonably well.

10. Ask students to give the directions to another student about where the money should be put and to whom it should be passed. For example, Saad says, " Maria, please give the dollar to Sachiko." Or Saad may say, " Maria, please put the dollar in your purse." (This generates a lot of laughter.)

11. Ask students to return all money to your desk. You have options here:
    If you're in a hurry, say, "Bring back all of my money!"
    If you want one more review, say, "Alicia, what do you have?" She answers. Say, "Please bring your _____ back to my desk."

Extensions:

1. Say, "I want to buy a pair of shoes for $26.66. What kind of money will I need?"

2. Elicit the answer: "A twenty-dollar bill, a five-dollar bill, a one-dollar bill, two quarters, a dime, a nickel, and a penny." (Expect to get the answer, "A credit card!") Join in the fun and continue with a different example.

3. Student volunteers take your place and ask the questions.

5.26 CHECKING THE WEATHER

Everyone talks about the weather; it's a great conversation starter. This routine gets students started on "weather" talk.

 **AIM:**   Reviewing weather vocabulary

Procedure:

1. Say, "Let's look at the weather today." Go to the window and say, "Oh, it's a nice day today. (or whatever the weather is) "It's warm here today. The sun is shining. It's a nice, warm day."

2. As you talk, write on the board a few possible phrases, for example: "It's warm. It's a nice day. The sun is shining."

3. Ask, "What is the weather like today, Maricia?" Get her response.

4. Repeat step 3 with several students.

5. Write on the board, "What is the weather like today?"

6. Then say, "Alexis, please ask Fredrico about the weather."

7. Start a chain in which the answerer (Fredrico) asks another student.

8. Continue the chain as long as there is interest. Students will use the answers on the board and perhaps other answers as well.

Note: If you do this routine for a few minutes every day, you can constantly introduce new vocabulary. Examples: It's very hot today. It's windy today; It might rain today, etc.

Extension: After your students have become familiar with the routine, you can add new weather locations and times. Ask them about their home countries. For example: "Do you think that it is a nice day in Sweden/Saudi Arabia/Columbia today?"

5.27 WHAT'S MY NUMBER?

Students really enjoy the movement and the variety of this exercise.

AIM: Review of numbers and arithmetic vocabulary

MATERIALS: tape, blank papers to make signs

Procedure:

1. Students form groups of seven.
2. Assign three random numbers to each of three students in each group. For example, one student gets a '7', one gets a '9', and another gets a '3'. Write these numbers on a piece of paper as you speak to the students. Students tape these signs to their chests.
3. Assign the roles of *plus sign* (+), *minus sign* (–), and *equals sign* (=) to three more students in each group. These signs are taped to their chests, also.
4. The remaining student in each group, the "answer person," has a blank sign.
5. Each group arranges itself in the shape of an arithmetic problem. Example: 9 – 7 + 3 = . (The "answer person" writes a 5 on his sign.)
6. Each group reads its problem to the whole class.
7. Groups rearrange themselves into new problems. (The answer person makes a new sign for each new answer.)
8. Continue the procedure as long as there is interest.

5.28 **WHAT WE KNOW**

This is a valuable activity for gathering words to use any way you want.

AIM: Vocabulary generating

Procedure:

1. Ask, "What do we already know about . . . "

2. As students call out words, list them on the board.

3. You can stop there, just using this quickly at the start or end of class. For example, on a Friday, ask, "What do we know about weekends?" Choose high-interest topics, like, "What do we know about tests?" Or you may:

   • sort the words into nouns and verbs

   • make sentences with the words

   • make vocabulary cards with the words

   • read something that includes the words

   • use the words as a base to teach other related words

After this activity, you may want to do "Vocabulary Cards," Chapter 5, page 85.

5.29 **HALF A PICTURE**

This activity is a way for students to say the words they know and learn new words. The whole class does it together, so if a student knows few or no words about the picture, that's okay.

AIM: Generating words to use in a later activity

MATERIALS: An interesting picture

Procedure:

1. Hold up the picture with half of it hidden.

2. With the whole class, talk about the half of the picture you can see. Write some of these words on the board.

3. Point to the hidden half and let your curiosity show. "What's in this half?"

4. As the class calls out ideas about what might be there, write their ideas on the board. (Offer prompts if they need help.)

5. Reveal the whole picture.

6. Erase ideas from the board that turned out not to be in the picture, talk about the guesses that were correct, and add new vocabulary that they didn't think of before.

7. Students copy these words into their notebooks.

5.30 VOCABULARY CHAIN

Challenge can be fun! In this activity students concentrate because they have to remember what others have said. This routine can be used with any content. For example:

> "Last Saturday I saw a movie." (to practice verbs)
> "Today I am wearing black pants." (to practice clothes)
> "I am going to buy apples." (to practice names of foods)

 **AIM:** Vocabulary development; reinforcing verb tenses by repeating a sentence frame many times

Procedure:

1. Students sit in a circle of no more than fifteen. In large classes, make several circles.

2. Choose a sentence to start the chain.

3. Say the sentence. For example, "Last Saturday I saw a movie."

4. Say, "Mohammed, what did I do?"

5. He answers, "You saw a movie."

6. Ask him, "What did *you* do?"

7. Mohammed answers, for example, "I went shopping." I help him form a complete sentence.

8. Point to the student next to Mohammed. Ask her, "What did I do?" She answers, "You saw a movie."

9. Indicate Mohammed. She says, "He went shopping."

10. Ask her, "What did *you* do?" She answers, for example, "I watched TV."

11. Indicate the next student in the circle. Point to those who already spoke as the new student repeats all the sentences in the chain.

12. Continue around the circle as the list of sentences gets longer and longer.

13. Elicit new verbs and different answers. No repeats.

14. Let students call, "Help!" if they don't remember a sentence.

15. Everyone applauds the last student, who had the hardest job!

Variation: For low beginners, rather than repeating whole sentences, use single vocabulary words. Practice colors, names, vegetables, furniture, or any vocabulary group.

5.31 WACKY PEOPLE

Students love to create these imaginary figures! They get excited as they find accessories to add on to the crazy figures.

AIM: Generating new vocabulary

MATERIALS: A stack of magazines, scissors (or students may tear out pictures), a large sheet of paper (12" x 18") for each group, glue or tape

Procedure:

1. In pairs or groups of three, students cut out people parts (facial features, parts of bodies). They also find clothing, parts of animals, and accessories (feathers, roller skates). Tell them, "Don't worry if you don't know the word. Just choose things you like." Students need not worry about keeping anything in proportion or being realistic; in fact, the crazier, the better!

2. They glue these onto their large paper, making a collage.

3. Students label as many parts as they can, writing the names on the collage. (With low beginners, you may provide most of the words.)

4. Groups visit other groups to add more labels to their collages. Circulate, helping where needed.

5. Everyone sits down in his/her group. Each group tells you a few interesting words from its collage (these may be new words). Write these words on the board.

6. As you go, ask, "Who else has a _____?" Talk about the words. You have options here:

    • Sort the words into categories, such as *old/new* or *facial features/accessories/clothing*.

    • Expand the words into phrases. For example, change *lips* to *large, red lips*.

    • Invite each group to come up and describe its collage to the whole class, naming as many things as they can.

7. Groups give their "wacky person" a name. Post the collages on the wall for all to admire.

8. Students walk around individually, copying into their notebooks a few more new words from the other collages.

Note: Save one wacky person collage in your files. Use it as an example to help a future class get started quickly.

There are many possible follow-ups. One is "Disappearing Vocabulary," Chapter 5, page 70.

Acknowledgment: We learned this activity from Ellen Abrams, who teaches art and Spanish at Roskruge Bilingual Elementary School in Tucson, Arizona.

Chapter Six

STRUCTURE

The grammar of a new language helps us to make sense of the new words and sounds. Putting words together in a meaningful structure helps us to learn and to remember. Grammar helps our students to see how their own language is similar and different from the target language. It puts structure into something that at first seems to be very complex and entangled. For example, grammar helps us to ask a question, make a negative remark, and put words in an order that our listener can understand. The activities in this chapter will help our students to feel at home in the structure of the new language.

6.1 BUILDING DIALOGUES ABOUT FOOD

We all enjoy good food. This activity helps to bring some of that enjoyment into the new language.

 **AIM:** Teaching food vocabulary and adjectives of taste; fluency practice; asking questions (both *yes/no* and information questions with *why*)

Procedure:

1. Write the names of several foods on the board. For example: *apples, carrots, bread, pizza, hamburger, eggs, soup, cheese, ice cream, chocolate.*

2. Explain meanings by mimicking, eliciting answers from students, and drawing on the board.

3. Ask, "Lucia, do you like bread?" Get her response and say, (while also writing this on the board) "Yes, I like bread."

4. Ask several more students and extend the question with, "Why do you like _____?" Elicit sentences like, "It tastes good."

5. Teach the words *sweet, sour, bitter,* and *salty* (put these words on the board) by acting them out and giving examples (*ice cream, lemons, strong coffee, potato chips*).

6. Ask, "Sofia, do you like ice cream?"

7. If she says, "Yes," ask her "Why?"

8. Write this sentence frame on the board: "I like _____ because it is _____."

9. Coach her to say, "I like ice cream because it is sweet."

10. Practice this pattern with several students.

11. Write on the board, "Do you like _____? Why do you like _____? I like _____ because _____."

12. Students stand and mingle, asking each other questions about foods and answering the questions.

13. Continue as long as there is interest.

14. Circulate among students, listening for correct questions and answers.

15. Ask, "Who remembers what Alicia likes?"

16. Students answer, "She likes _____." This gives the lesson an added dimension: pronouns and the third-person singular 's'.

6.2   WHAT DO WE DO?

In this activity students learn something about their classmates while practicing question formation and *do* and *does*, which need a great deal of practice and review.

AIM: Practicing *do* and *does*, using questions, reviewing verbs and introducing new ones; practicing short answers and negatives

MATERIALS: A few pictures large enough for the whole class to see

Procedure:

1. Say, "I am a teacher. I do many things. I teach English. I talk. I cook food. I ride a bicycle," etc. Mime as you talk.

2. Invite a student to the front of the class and ask, "Mohammed, do you speak Arabic?" Elicit his answer and repeat it, "Mohammed speaks Arabic."

3. Ask the class, "Does Mohammed speak Arabic?" Elicit, "Yes, he does."

4. Repeat steps 2 and 3, eliciting a few more answers from Mohammed about what he does. As you go along, write the simple form of each verb under Mohammed's name on the board.

5. Invite a non-Arab student up, and ask what he/she does. Repeat steps 2 and 3 until you have a few verbs under his/her name on the board. Be sure that at least one answer contrasts with Mohammed's. (For example, "Does Sonia speak Arabic?" Elicit from the class, "No, she doesn't.") This will introduce the negative *doesn't* into your lesson.

6. Play with comparisons, eliciting choral repetition and individual repetition. Introduce new pronouns as you need them. For example, "Sonia rides a bike. Does Mohammed ride a bike?" The class says, "No, he doesn't!" "Mohammed does homework. Sonia does homework, too. Do they do homework?" The class answers, "Yes, they do!"

7. Continue with a few more students.

8. If you want some different verbs, show a picture of just about anything. For example: a bird, a doctor, or a secretary.

9. Ask, "What does a bird do?" Elicit verbs like, "flies, eats bugs, lays eggs." Write the simple forms of these verbs on the board under *bird*.

10. Repeat step 6 with the new verbs.

11. Write this dialogue frame on the board:

> "Does a _____ _____?"
>
> (verb)
>
> "Yes, he/she/it/they _____." or "No, he/she/it/
> they_____."

12. In pairs, students ask each other questions to review *yes/no* questions and answers.

13. Circulate to be sure they are using the sentence frames correctly.

14. Students write three sentences about what they *do*, using verbs from the board. For example:

> "I ride a bicycle."
> "I speak Japanese."
> "I drive a car."

15. Students write three sentences about things they *don't* do. For example:

> "I don't eat bugs."
> "I don't smoke."
> "I don't drink coffee."

Extension:

1. Collect the papers.

2. The next day, give each paper to someone else, not the writer.

3. Students write on this paper, for example:

> Hisashi rides a bicycle.   He does not eat bugs.
> He speaks Japanese.   He does not smoke.
> He drives a car.   He does not drink coffee.

4. Students walk around and tell each other about their classmates.

6.3 CLEANING UP THE MESS

Everyone knows what a joy it is to get one's messy room cleaned up. In this activity students practice the past tense with the clean-up job.

AIM: Past tense verbs, vocabulary development

MATERIALS: One copy of the picture for each pair of students

Procedure:

1. While looking at the messy room, elicit descriptive words and write them on the board.

2. Direct students' attention to the clean room and ask, "What happened?"

3. Elicit or provide: "Someone cleaned the room."

4. Ask, "What did someone do?"

5. Elicit sentences that complete the clean-up and write these on the board. ("He/she picked up the book, put away the shoes, watered the flower, made the bed, straightened the picture," etc.)

6. Students repeat each sentence chorally and individually.

7. In pairs, students take turns saying the sentences to each other.

8. (Optional step for low beginners) Students copy the sentences on paper.

9. Erase a key word from each sentence on the board. (This can be the verb or the household item.)

10. Students turn over their papers and re-create the sentences. (Peeking at the other side or at a neighbor's paper is okay!)

11. To check for correctness, students leave their papers, move to a different desk, sit down there, and check that paper.

12. Send a student to the board. The class tells him/her what words to put back in the blanks.

Variation: Use this routine with any two things that can be compared or contrasted. For example:

- someone dressed for a party and someone dressed for a picnic
- someone at home and someone at work
- a table set for a simple meal and a table set for a banquet
- a rural landscape and a cityscape

6.4 WHAT IS A NOUN? PART I

This is a good activity for low beginners and a quick review for others.

AIM: Learning what is and what is not a noun, learning the categories of nouns

Procedure:

1. Ask the students, "What is a noun?" and see what they can answer. Let anyone who wants to answer do so. Maybe several students will shout out different words, like *cat, girl, student,* or *book.*

2. Write these on the board in three columns. *Girl* and *student* will go in the same column.

3. If students answer *person* or *place* write those words at the top of the columns.

4. Keep encouraging responses until you have words in these 5 columns: *person, animal, place, thing,* and *idea* (*idea* is by far the most difficult, and, for beginners, much more emphasis should be placed on the other categories). When you finish, you should have something like this on the board:

person	animal	place	thing	idea
teacher	cat	city	bus	love
student	dog	school	car	fear
doctor	cow	hospital	desk	freedom
girl	bird	supermarket	pencil	
woman	fish	home	sandwich	

5. Write a sentence like the following on the board and ask a student to put in the correct words: "The _____ eats a _____ everyday."

6. Students can use words from the list or come up with their own ideas, as long as the words make sense. Here are some more sentence frames:

   "The _____ goes to the _____ every Saturday."

   "The _____ talks to the _____ every day."

"_____ is for all people."

"The _____ is on the _____."

7. Continue until most students are putting appropriate nouns in the blanks.

See "What is a Noun? Part II," below, for a follow-up activity.

6.5 WHAT IS A NOUN? PART II

This is a game of putting the correct noun in the correct category as fast as possible. You can use the list of nouns from "What is a Noun? Part I" if you want.

If your students do not understand clearly what a noun is, do "What Is A Noun? Part I," on the previous page, before this activity.

AIM: Becoming familiar with nouns

MATERIALS: Slips of paper, tape

Procedure:

There are several ways to do this activity:

1. Write all the nouns on separate slips of paper before the class begins.
2. Hand the slips out to the students until all slips are in students' hands. Write the following noun categories on the board: *person, animal, place, thing, idea.*
3. Say, "Go" and all students run up and tape the nouns in the right category. The whole class checks to see if the nouns are in the right columns.

Variation One: If there is no time to write out the slips of paper, this can be a dictation.

1. Write the five categories on the board as column headings.
2. Students copy this on a piece of paper.
3. Dictate nouns. As you say each word, students write it on their papers in the correct columns.
4. Students exchange papers to check each other's work as you write the nouns on the board.

Variation Two:

MATERIALS: Soft, easy-to-catch ball or stuffed animal to toss to students

1. A volunteer stands at the board, ready to write nouns in their correct places as classmates say them.
2. Throw the ball to a student and say, for example,"Your word is airplane."
3. The student says, "Thing."
4. The scribe writes *airplane* under the heading *thing*.
5. The student with the ball tosses it to another student and you say another word. The game continues until all the words are in their correct categories.

Extension: After students are clear about what a noun is, add an occasional adjective or verb. Ask, with disbelief in your voice, "Is this a *person*? Is this an *animal*? a *place*? *thing*? *idea*? Let them put the words that are *not* nouns in a column headed *other words*.

6.6   QUESTIONS AND ANSWERS—SPEAKING

Students literally think on their feet as they learn the meanings of question words by matching them with appropriate answers. This activity helps you and your students see what they already know and what they need to practice more.

AIM: Learning what answers are appropriate to particular question words

MATERIALS: 3" x 5" cards or pieces of paper, tape

Procedure:

1. Write a few question words or phrases, each on a separate card. For example: *do, how much, who, when, where, why, how, does, what time, how many, is, are.*
2. Tape the cards around the room. You will post a card on the wall for each student in your class, repeating some question words if necessary.

3. Write an answer to one of the question words on a card and hand it to a student. For example, if you are practicing *do, how much, who,* and *when,* give these four answer cards to four different students:

| yes | | $7.00 | | Victor | | 3:00 pm |

4. Make more answer cards (different answers to the same question words). Give these cards to other students.

5. Do this for all the students and tell them to walk around the room and look for the question word that matches their answer card.

6. When they have found their match, they tape their answer card under the question word.

7. Everyone continues circulating, reading, discussing and checking for accuracy until all question words and answer cards are matched.

8. Students stand next to a question/answer they like. Let them mill around until each student is standing next to a question/answer.

9. Call on a student to ask the person standing to their left a complete question with his/her word. For example, if their question word is *do,* they ask, "Do you study English every day?"

10. The student on the left answers with a complete sentence, using the answer word, for example: "Yes, I do."

11. The question-and-answer chain continues. The student who answered looks at his/her question word and asks a complete question of the person on the left, who provides the answer.

12. As this continues, with students asking and answering, all the other students listen and provide help as needed for the two who are speaking.

Note: Save the question and answer cards to use again.

See "Questions and Answers—Writing," Chapter 4, page 59, for an activity that extends this into writing complete sentences.

6.7   THINK FAST! PRACTICING VERB TENSES

Being able to produce spur-of-the-moment oral sentences gives students a real sense of accomplishment. This activity can be used for as many verb tenses as your class has studied.

AIM: Reviewing verb tenses

MATERIAL: (Optional) A soft, easy-to-catch ball for students to toss to each other

Procedure:

1. Write the verb tenses to be reviewed on the board. For example: present, past, present continuous.

2. Have a certain verb in mind, such as walk.

3. Toss the ball to (or call on) a student and say, "Tell me a sentence with walk in this tense."

4. Point to a tense on the board.

5. Wait for the student to think. If he/she produces a good sentence, go to step 7. If, after a few moments, the student is having trouble, tell him/her to throw the ball to, or call on a friend to help and continue to step 6.

6. Two students are now trying to produce a sentence. If they say a good sentence, go to step 7. If not, they may get a third person to help, or the whole class may help. When a good sentence is produced, go to step 7.

7. The person holding the ball tosses it to a new student, and the game begins again.

8. Say, "Tell me a sentence with _____ (choose another verb) in this tense."

9. Point to a tense on the board.

10. Continue as long as interest is high.

Variation: This routine can be used for many different grammar points. Try this one, then create more of your own!

To practice third person singular 's':

- Write pronouns on the board, for example: *I, you, he, she, it, we, you, they.*

- Give a student a verb, for example, *walk*, while pointing to a pronoun.
- The student says, for example, "He walks."
- If you want more information, put a "+" on the board and point to it.
- The student says, for example, "He walks to the supermarket."

Note: This activity can be tailored to each class or individual problem area in verb tenses.

6.8   WHEN SUDDENLY . . .

After students have studied the present continuous tense, they often become curious about the past continuous. This activity provides a good introduction and a good recycling of the past tense.

AIM: Introducing and/or practicing the past continuous and simple past tenses

Procedure:

1. Say, "I am going to tell you a story about what happened to me last weekend."

2. Begin your story with something like this: "I went for a long walk in the mountains. I was very happy to be outside. I was walking along, when suddenly . . ." Pause for drama.

3. Continue, "A bear jumped in front of me! I ran. The bear ran, too. The bear and I were running, when suddenly . . ." Pause to see if any student comes up with information to finish the sentence. If not, you provide an ending, "We fell into a big hole."

4. On the board, write the short story that you have just told.

5. As a whole class, discuss the tenses and when to use them. (We use the past continuous tense when a longer-lasting action in the past is interrupted by a short action, etc.)

6. Choose one student and help him/her get started telling a story using the formula of your story, for example: "Last weekend I was sitting in my chair thinking, when suddenly . . ."

7. The next student continues the sentence, using a verb in the simple past tense, for example: "A bird flew in the window."

8. Another student uses the same verb *flew*, but now in the past continuous: "The bird was flying in the window when suddenly . . ."

9. Another student finishes the sentence with a new verb in the past tense, for example: "The telephone rang."

10. Continue until all students have had a chance to produce at least one sentence. If the meaning becomes too strange, help by providing a verb, or start over with a new idea.

6.9 THIS IS MY RED ELEPHANT

Students really remember this hands-on introduction to possessive adjectives. It has the added bonus of teaching *this, that, these, those,* and new vocabulary.

AIM: Introducing and/or practicing possessive adjectives; expanding vocabulary

MATERIALS: Bring something that the students can claim as their own. Stuffed animals are extremely good because they are so silly. Plastic food is also good. Pictures will work if that's all you have, but think creatively!

Procedure:

1. Give each student a different object.

2. Give yourself an object, such as "a red elephant."

3. If the names of the objects are new to the students, list all of them on the board.

4. Say to the class, "This is *my* red elephant."

5. Point to the object that a student is holding and say, "That is *your* brown monkey."

6. Repeat, "This is *my* red elephant. That is *your* brown monkey."

7. Ask the student, "What is that?"

8. The student answers, "This is *my* brown monkey." (If he/she gets the possessive adjective wrong, invite classmates to help him/her.)

9. Ask the student, "What is this?"

10. The student answers, "That is *your* red elephant."

11. The student then says, "This is *my* brown monkey," and asks another student, "What is that?"

12. Student Two answers, "This is *my* _____ _____. That is *your* _____ _____."

13. After several students have asked and answered the questions, and the whole class seems to understand *my* and *your*, point to a student's object in the class and ask the other students, "What is that?"

14. Students answer chorally, "That is *her* (or *his*) _____ _____." (You may need to tell them what to say the first few times.)

15. Point to other students' objects and let the class provide the sentences, using *her*, *his*, *my* and *your* until all students seem to understand.

16. Introduce *their* and *our* by pointing to several students and their objects and saying,

    "*Their* _____ are _____." (for example: "*Their* animals are small.")

    "*Our* _____ are _____." (for example: "*Our* animals are brown.")

    "*Our* _____ have _____." (for example: "*Our* animals have big ears.")

17. Put new vocabulary on the board as it comes up.

18. Students continue to practice together or in small groups.

6.10 WHAT AHMED DOES

AIM: Practicing third person 's'

Procedure:

1. Write on the board, "What do I do that takes money?"

2. Write a true answer, for example, "I buy old furniture."

3. Ask, "What do *you* do that takes money?" Elicit a few answers.

4. Students write their personal answer.

5. Erase the board and write this model interview:

> Student 1: "What do you do that takes money?"
>
> Student 2: "I _____."

6. Bring one student up to demonstrate the interview with you:

> Ask the question.
> The whole class repeats.
> The student gives his/her answer.
> The whole class repeats.

7. Students copy the model down on paper.

8. On the same paper, students write two or three other things they do.

9. Students turn the paper face down on their desks.

10. Erase the model interview.

11. Practice the model a few more times, chorally and individually, until students are speaking confidently.

12. Students interview each other in pairs about the two or three things they wrote earlier. (If you hear errors as you walk around, ask them to check their model. Then they should turn their paper face down again.)

13. Students write a few sentences about their partner. For example: "Ahmed plays soccer."

14. Pairs combine to make groups of four. They take turns telling their new partners what they learned about their original partner. (They should work without the paper, if possible.) Encourage listeners to insist on the necessary third person 's'.

15. In plenary, ask, "Who remembers something about somebody?"

16. Students call out what they remember. For example:

"Raul buys shoes."

"Junko goes to the gym."

17. (Optional) On the board, write:

"Me, too!"

"So do I!"

18. Demonstrate how students can use these two phrases.

Note: For step one, students may use dictionaries if necessary, or ask you or their classmates for help.

Variations:

1. Repeat this activity on other days, using different categories. For example, "What do you do . . . ?"

alone

with one other person

with a group of friends

at home

at school

2. Once your class has done this, it can become a quick warm-up activity or something you do in the last five minutes of class.

3. Change this to the past tense by asking, "What did you do last week that cost money?"

6.11 WHAT YOU DO WITH A BIKE

In this activity, students have to think about which verbs can go with which nouns while they make real statements about real classmates. They learn vocabulary because they make meaningful associations with each word.

 **AIM:** Vocabulary expansion, verb tense practice, learning which nouns and verbs can go together

Procedure:

1. Divide students into team A and team B, and count off within each team.

2. Student A1 makes a statement about a classmate, using "has." For example, "Maria has a bike." (Give help if needed.)

3. Ask, "What does Maria do with the bike?" Student B1 uses another verb to make a sentence with the same subject and object. For example, "Maria rides the bike," or "Maria likes the bike."

4. The game continues. A2 makes a sentence about a classmate, using "has," and B2 adds a sentence with a different verb. For example: A1: "Masanori has a dog." B2: "Masanori plays with the dog." Then A3 and B3 take a turn, and so on.

5. After each sentence, ask listening students whether it is correct.

Note: For low beginning classes, make a chart on the board that includes several things your students have and a few verbs that can go with each one. Ask your students for ideas. Here's the start of such a chart:

What we have	What we do
glasses	wear, put on, take off
pencil	write with, drop, lose, break
mother	love, help

Variations:

1. For large classes, model with a few students in front of the room, then divide students into groups of ten (five A's and five

B's). Assign one or two of your more advanced students to guide each group.

2. For extra playfulness, encourage B students to make some sentences reasonable and others silly. For example, they may say "Maria rides the bike" or "Maria eats the bike." The A team must decide whether the sentence is reasonable or silly.

Extensions:

1. After students are doing this basic game well, add pronouns. For example: "Maria has a bike. She rides the bike."

2. Later, when you teach the possessive adjectives *his* and *her*, play this game again. For example: "Maria has a bike. She rides her bike."

6.12 PREPOSITION PICTURES

This activity enlists peer support in using prepositions of place correctly. Drawing pictures reinforces learning through physical action. Don't worry if some students say they can't draw; just put some very basic stick figures on the board and tell them, "If you can do this, it's fine!"

AIM: Practicing prepositions of place

Procedure:

1. Dictate sentences with prepositions of place. For example: "The monkey jumps into the box."

2. Each student draws what he/she hears.

3. In pairs or small groups, students compare their pictures. If they want to, they may change their drawing.

4. Each student now writes, under the picture, the sentence as he/she remembers it.

5. You have a choice for the next step:

    • Call on students to dictate their sentences to you. Write some of these on the board. Correct errors as needed. If the wrong preposition shows up in a sentence, draw a picture of what that would mean.

    • Send all the students to the board in pairs. Student A reads his/her sentence and student B draws what he/she hears. Then student B reads his/her sentence and student A draws what he/she hears. Circulate, helping as necessary.

Note: If students forget to use the third-person 's' (writing, for example, "The monkey jump into the box"), ask classmates to add the necessary 's.'

Use the activity, "What Ahmed Does," Chapter 6, page 117, as a warm-up a couple of times a week to practice this 's' ending.

6.13 CAN YOU GO?

This activity teaches the importance of articles and prepositions. Many students see articles as meaningless, but here, they see that one little *the* can mean the difference between life and death! This particular special use of "the" is not very important, but we like this activity because it helps students notice when "the" is present in a sentence and when it is not. Subliminally, students are also learning the use of *Can you_____?* and *your.*

 **AIM:** Listening, prepositions of place, articles

Procedure:

1. Draw a picture of a car on the board. Each student copies it, putting it in the middle of a piece of paper.

2. Each student draws a little picture (less than one inch high) of someone he/she loves. For example, "your baby brother."

They cut or tear this out so they can move it around.

3. Say, "Put your baby brother in front of the car." Students look at classmates' papers until all have the baby in the right place.

4. Ask, "Can you go?" Students should answer with a resounding "No!" (If any students are silent, ask the question again and again until every student is responding.)

5. Say, "Put your baby brother in the front of the car. Can you go?" Because you said "the," students should move the baby to the front seat, inside the car. Teach this point, then repeat the question. Students say, "Yes!" Write these two instructions (steps 3 and 5) on the board.

6. Alternate these two commands, each time asking, "Can you go?" until all students hear whether or not you said "the" and are moving the baby to the right place and answering *yes* or *no* correctly without looking at others' papers.

7. Begin adding other commands. Keep recycling commands the students have already mastered as you go along. Wait for a 90% correct response rate among your students before adding each new command so that students will have fun and gain confidence. Here are the commands you can add:

> "Put your baby brother in back of the car."
> "Put your baby brother in the back of the car."
> "Put your baby brother on the front of the car."
> "Put your baby brother on the back of the car."

Acknowledgement: This activity is a variation of one we learned from Dawn Essman, who teaches at Pima Community College in Tucson, Arizona.

6.14 SCHOOL SUPPLIES

All those familiar school supplies have names, and students want to know what they are! This activity will help them learn the names while practicing other parts of the language as well.

AIM: Reviewing prepositions of location, subject pronouns, present tense with *be* and *have*, demonstrative pronouns *this, that, these, those,* teaching names of school supplies, review of names

MATERIALS: A bag full of school supplies—all the supplies you have in your desk (for example: paperclips, pencils, paper, pen, stapler, tape, eraser, ruler, scissors, envelope, white-out, glue, staples, push pins, thumb-tacks, computer disks). Have one item for each student in your class. Borrow items from other teachers if you don't have enough. Items can be duplicated.

Procedure:

1. Call the students to your desk and give an item to each student, carefully saying the name of the item and asking the student to repeat the name of the item to the whole class. (You may write the words on the board.) Example:

   > Teacher: "This is a stapler. I am giving Sonia the stapler. Sonia, What do you have?"
   > Sonia: "I have a stapler."

2. Students call out their name and their item. Example: "I am Rami and I have a ruler."

3. Students call out the names of other students and their items. Example: "Abdullah has tape. Lise has paperclips."

4. Collect all the items on the desk.

5. Volunteers come to the desk and review all the items.

6. If students need the support, you may write prepositions of location on the board (for example: *behind, in front of, in the middle, under, on top of*).

7. Say, "Now I want to make my desk look nice and organized. Where should I put the tape?"

8. Students call out directions. For example: "Put the stapler on the desk. Put the book under the stapler."

9. Follow their directions with each item, helping with prepositions when needed.

10. This requires some acting, as you place and replace materials according to student directions. (There is always a lot of fun during this phase as students get mixed up and you repeat, "You want me to put this big book *in* the eraser? Do you really mean that?")

11. A volunteer student takes over your role of desk organizer, and the activity continues as long as there is interest.

12. In pairs, students chose five to ten desk items—the things they most need on their desk.

13. Together they write sentences explaining where they want these things on their desk.

Variation: The same activity can be done with personal items contributed by students (for example: lipstick, mirror, penknife, medicine bottle, diary, matches, cigarette-case etc.)

6.15 QUESTIONS ABOUT ME

In a language class, students work a lot better when they get to know each other. This activity helps!

AIM: Fluency practice, question formation review

Procedure:

Write the name of an American president or another well-known person on the board together with some well-known facts about this person. Example: *President Kennedy; The White House; John; Jacqueline; Boston; Harvard; two children; Caroline; John.*

1. Point to one fact on the board and say, "This is the answer. What is the question?"

2. Volunteers help to make the question and other volunteers write the question on the board.

3. Repeat the procedure with the other answers on the board.

4. Review by having half of the class ask the questions chorally and the other half answer them. Then switch.

5. Write similar answers about yourself on the board. These answers could include the number of your age; the place you were born; the number of years you have been a teacher; the

names of your children; the number of rooms in your house; your street address; the word *yes* and the word *no*. Use your imagination.

6. Volunteers produce questions.

7. Other volunteers write the questions on the board. Help with corrections as needed.

8. At the board or on paper, students write answers about themselves.

9. Circulate to help with spelling and vocabulary.

10. Working in pairs, students ask questions about their partners' answers.

11. Students switch partners and continue the activity.

12. Students can switch partners many times for as long as the activity holds interest for them.

13. Students return to their own desks and individually write out three questions. For example:

    "Where were you born?"

    "What is your address?"

14. Students find a partner they haven't spoken to before. They read their questions to their new partner and write the answers.

Extension: If you wish to use this as the basis for a writing assignment, students can write a short composition about their partner. After these compositions are corrected, you might post them on the walls.

6.16 TELL IT LIKE IT ISN'T

Students can laugh at mistakes by the teacher in this lively activity. It also generates a nice list of action verbs you can save to use at some other time.

AIM: Practicing the present continuous, action verbs, and negation

Procedure:

1. Take a student where others can't hear, and whisper to him or her to mime an action such as "Eat a sandwich."

2. As the student mimes for the class, say, "Carlos is driving a car. Right?" Put *drive* on the board as you say this.

3. Elicit from students, "No, he is not driving a car. He is eating a sandwich." Put *eat* on the board.

4. Ask another student to come to the front. Again, whisper a suggested action. (Possibilities include *eating, drinking, cooking, brushing teeth, sleeping, driving, reading, writing, taking a shower, turning on a shower, walking,* etc.)

5. Continue adding to the list of verbs on the board as the activity goes along.

6. Repeat with more students. Each time, suggest the wrong answer and have the class correct you.

Extension: For more advanced beginners, call on student volunteers to suggest the wrong answers. The class corrects them.

TO THE INDEXES . . .

CODE TO CHAPTERS

1   Listening

2   Speaking

3   Reading

4   Writing

5   Vocabulary

6   Structure

GENERAL INDEX OF ACTIVITIES
All Content

These activities are excellent for teaching any vocabulary set: foods, colors, clothing, parts of the body, days, months, numbers, etc.

Alphabet

Students learn their ABC's and more with these activities!

Body Parts

These activities make learning body parts an "earful" of fun!

Class Cohesion

When students know each other well, they are less nervous about making mistakes and more ready to communicate in their new language. These activities help!

Colors

You will find many more ways of teaching colors under the index category "All Content."

Competitive Games

These activities can focus students' attention and add to the fun.

Correcting Errors

Students want to "get it right." Here are some supportive ways to help them.

Dialogues

These activities give students a head start on their conversation skills.

Directions/Locations

You will find many more ways of teaching directions and locations under the index category "All Content."

Discussion Starters

These activities give students plenty to talk about!

Drawing

Drawing allows students to play with meaning when they aren't yet ready to speak much.

Energizers

When students are tired, try these activities to add some pep and energy to your lessons!

First Few Days

People new to a language may have some anxieties about it. These activities are low-stress and build students' confidence in their ability to learn this new language.

Foods

You will find many more ways of teaching foods under the index category "All Content."

Household Things

You will find many more ways of teaching household things under the index category "All Content."

Low Beginners

Most of the activities in this book are easily adapted for the full range of beginning students. You can use them with low beginners if you control content and vocabulary. We have indexed here those activities that are already suitable for low beginning students.

Money

You will find many more ways of teaching money under the index category "All Content."

Months of the Year

You will find many more ways of teaching months under the index category "All Content."

Music or Song

People remember the language they learn in songs, and the pleasure of songs increases motivation!

Numbers

You will find many more ways of teaching numbers in the index category "All Content."

Personal Items

You will find many more ways of teaching personal items under the index category "All Content."

Physical Movement

Students remember language better when movement accompanies it. They also have a good time! These activities get everyone moving!

Pictures

One picture is worth a thousand words to beginners. Pictures make the meaning clear when words alone are not enough. Following are activities using pictures.

Polite Phrases

These are the first things people need in a new language.

Preview

Students take more pleasure in reading/listening when they know in advance what they will read/listen to. This is even more essential with beginners: when you pre-teach what they will read/listen to, they do the main activity with joy.

Pronunciation

Real Objects

Bringing objects into class adds excitement and an element of reality. It also supports meaning, which is essential in a beginning class!

Review

Recycling language is essential with beginners, but it must be done with variety so that student interest remains high. These activities provide what your students need.

Settling Down

Try these activities if your students need to settle down and focus their attention.

Short

Are you waiting for a few late students? Do you have a few extra minutes at the end of a class? Try these!

Spelling

Seasons

You will find many more ways of teaching seasons under the index category "All Content."

Weather

You will find many more ways of teaching weather under the index category "All Content."

ALPHABETICAL INDEX OF ACTIVITIES

Quick Notes

Quick Notes